Dreaming the Iron Dream

Collected Racial and Political Essays of Harold A. Covington

Liberty Bell Publications

ISBN 1-59364-025-0

Library of Congress Control Number: 2004117676

Copyright © 2005

by Harold A. Covington

Printed in the United States of America

Liberty Bell Publications
P.O. Box 890
York, SC 29745
libertybellpublications. com

Contents

Introduction

Greetings to Mr. and Mrs. America, and all the ships at sea.

These essays, or monologues, or rants, or whatever you want to call them, come from what has been up until now my most productive period polemic-wise, the Nineties and the early Oughts. They are what is known in Russian as *samisdat,* unauthorized dissident political and social commentaries transmitted by a kind of literary underground to a small number of readers by whatever means come to hand. The earlier pieces come from a weekly newsletter which I published throughout most of the Nineties called *Resistance,* which was a true samisdat publication—small, crudely typed, and reproduced in the cheapest copy shops or in some cases surreptitiously run off on the copy machines at whatever lowly temporary job I was working at the time to keep out of the homeless shelter. The later raves are, of course, from that great purveyor of samisdat in our time, the internet.

Other than some passing references in some of the later articles, I have deliberately excluded most of my Northwest Migration material. The purpose of this anthology is to provide readers with the best of HAC in the pre-Northwest sense; my Northwest Homeland raves will be collected together and melded into one long, stripped-down polemic at a later date, our little white book, so to speak. This collection is frankly a convenience for me, to obviate the necessity of my sending out reams of increasingly aging material to new people. The monologues I have included are in my view the best of my febrile crop, plus several which I added by request from readers, such as *How NOT To Do It* and *Our Socialism.* I tried to make a selection that wouldn't be too redundant. The Movement being what it is, I have to use a lot of spaced repetition. The monologues are arranged in approximate chronological order. For the record, as far as conveying what I want to convey to our people, my favorites are *The Song, Not The Singer; Dreaming the Iron Dream;* and *But Harold, What Do You Want Us To DO?*

Enjoy!

-HAC
Olympia, Washington
October 2004

[August 1992]

"The Mountain Has Fallen…"
Harold Covington's funeral oration for Robert Miles

On August 16th, 1992, a giant departed from among us when Robert Miles died at the age of 67, three months to the day after the death of his beloved wife, Dorothy. The gap which he has left in our ranks will not easily be filled.

For over forty years, Bob Miles played a leading role in the White resistance movement in America, his courage and vision earning him worldwide renown among every friend and foe alike of Aryan man. Bob endured repeated assault; a life of grim poverty and unremitting hardship; six years of false imprisonment on perjured testimony in the worst hellhole of America's prison system as well as a disgraceful attempt in 1987 to imprison him yet again on bogus sedition charges; decades of spying and harassment; the imprisonment and murder of friends and family members; and an avalanche of media abuse and defamation without parallel in the annals of gutter journalism.

They never broke him. Bob Miles met and overcame every attack, every ordeal which this evil regime inflicted on him, and he did so with a calm courage, a quiet dignity, and an irrepressible charm and humor which, more than anything else Bob did or said or wrote, drove the Jews and their lickspittle lackeys in the United States government to enraged distraction.

Bob Miles clearly understood something which many in our Movement have lost sight of, which is that *death is no big deal.* It is an inevitable fact of existence, to be accepted philosophically and met with dignity when the time comes. What matters is how one *lives,* what one leaves behind in the way of accumulated knowledge, experience, and moral example. For all of us today and for comrades of the future, role models don't come any stronger or more admirable than Bob Miles.

More than any White racial nationalist patriot in contemporary times, Bob *lived* his simple, powerful philosophy, which he sometimes referred to by the Irish Gaelic name of Sinn Fein, "Ourselves Alone". To Bob it was all very straightforward. Aryan man is the pinnacle of God's creation; we don't *need* anything which any other race or culture can offer us in exchange for admixture. All that is necessary to preserve our race and ensure a future for our seed among the stars is a simple recognition of who we are, and the spiritual willpower to just say no to every poisoned chalice, every rotten sweetmeat of which the Jew urges us to partake.

Bob understood the one basic principle which holds the key to our entire struggle, yet which seems so incredibly difficult for many of us to grasp; which indeed, some of us never succeed in grasping. *The Jews are not the problem,* nor are the blacks or the Hispanics or the politicians or the international bankers or the Communists or any other grouping of our racial adversaries. *We* are the problem. Our weakness, our laziness, our profound moral cowardice, our craven unwillingness to place our physical bodies and our creature comforts at risk, as Bob himself did without fear or hesitation.

When we look in a mirror, there we see our enemy. But if we look hard enough, we can see Bob Miles standing behind us, a smile on his face and his hand on our shoulder to guide and uplift and strengthen us, as ever he did when he was with us here in life.

In ancient Celtic times, when a High King of Tara died, messengers were dispatched in swift chariots riding the length and breadth of all Ireland, from Antrim in the north to Kerry in the southwest. At each village and crossroads and castle they came to, these couriers cried out, *"The mountain has fallen!"*

Our mountain has fallen, but his spirit lives on, and it is strong.

[April 1993]

Adolf Hitler: A Personal Testament

I have always known that Hitler was right. Even when I was a child and had no idea what National Socialism was all about, I seemed to have an instinctive recognition that all was not right in the society I was growing up in, and that anyone whom the authorities of that society feared, hated, and reviled as much as Adolf Hitler had to have something going for him.

When I played army with the other boys in my Burlington, North Carolina neighborhood, I always wanted to fight on the German side. Nor was this unusual; there were other boys like myself who drew swastikas on their schoolbook covers and rooted for the Germans when watching television shows like *Combat* or *The Gallant Men.* There was something in the shape of that Teutonic coal-scuttle helmet that thrilled our very souls. I have often wondered how this could be, when we were so young we could have no idea of the issues involved with the war or what the NSDAP was all about, and indeed were constantly subjected to a barrage of anti-NS propaganda, in a time when the war was a very recent memory. I think that this was because there is a kind of innate moral faculty in our people which Aryans are born with, which instinctively recognizes the difference between truth and lies, between right and wrong. It's a pity more of us can't retain that faculty into our adult lives.

Once I grew old enough to begin to understand things a bit, my earlier childish admiration and fascination with the Third Reich and the dynamic figure of Adolf Hitler grew, as I came to realize that my initial instincts had been correct. For one thing, even as a child reading my first books on the Second World War, I never bought into the Holocaust myth. I had no idea what the word "logistics" meant, but the idea that a nation fighting for its very existence would devote immense resources, manpower, and time to a pointless act of mass extermination was palpably ridiculous. I

9

wrote the Holocaust story off as typical war propaganda and read on.

When I was about ten, I met my first German war veteran, a friend of a friend of our family, a handsome and talented middle-aged artist from Greensboro whom I will call Johann, in case he still lives. I didn't know it, but Johann had been a *Fallschirmjäger* during the war. At a cocktail party one night some loud-mouthed redneck was holding forth on how he'd whupped up on ole Hitler and won the war singlehandedly. He was describing some battle in Italy and said, "...Then the gawd damn Natsy paratroopers come rainin' down outen the sky!"

Johann spoke up quietly from his corner. *"Ja,"* he said. "I remember. Ve jumped on you. You ran avay." The redneck fool was noticeably silent for the rest of the evening.

I was fascinated. Here was a man who had actually worn that helmet, that uniform with the eagle and swastika I had seen so often in movies and on TV. As soon as I could, I got Johann off to one side and asked him eagerly, "Did you ever meet Adolf Hitler?"

"No, not personally," he replied with a smile. "But I saw him many times. I am from Nuremberg, where they had the big rallies, and every year the Führer would drive beneath the window of my house in his open car. Once he looked up and saw me in the window and smiled. Later on I was a Hitler Youth, and I heard him speak." Johann was silent for a while, then said, "When you heard his words, you knew there was a God." Years later, I heard the words of Adolf Hitler, and I knew. I hear them still.

Gimme That Ole Time Religion

From the misty mountain passes of West Virginia the terrible tale was whispered. The rumor traveled at the speed of light along telephone lines, faster than Benny Klassen running from a subpoena. It moseyed along at the speed of a snail through the postal system. The sordid smear oozed into every nook and cranny of the Movement, hanging in the air like the fetid stench of Tom Metzger's socks. Upon hearing it dogs howled, strong men trembled, and white-headed little old ladies in tennis shoes saw terrible omens in the froth of their beer.

The Scribe's enemies cackled with glee. Surely this would do the trick! The upstart would be crushed! No longer would anyone dare to question what the Great White Leaders do with their supporters' donation money! No longer would the skeletons in a dozen closets be rattled once a month by this impertinent jackanapes from Carolina. For the secret was out! All was revealed! Verily, the word hath come down from on high, from the Olympian sanctum of the Great Man Himself through his chosen acolyte, Willard! Dare we utter it? Dare we whisper the doleful tidings?

"Harold Covington is secretly a....a...a *Christian!"*

Fire! Eclipse! Blue ruin!

There you have it, folks. I am accused of adherence to the religion which inspired the Crusaders to march all the way to Palestine, pausing en route ethnically to cleanse whole districts of Europe of Jews, overcoming awesome obstacles and grim hardships, until they stormed Jerusalem and slaughtered Semites as Tancred and Godfrey de Bouillon rode through the streets up to their horses' knees in non-White blood. What kind of Aryan could possibly admire such an insipid faith? I am accused of entertaining fond thoughts towards the God to whom the Afrikaners prayed on the Day of the Covenant in 1836, before rising to

11

their feet and smashing the Zulu impis into the dust at Blood River. They promised to build a church if their "Jewish" deity gave them victory. I have walked through that simple, powerfully moving Church of the Covenant, in Pietermaritzburg. Yep, got me cold on that one, Willard! I am indicted on suspicion of respect for the faith which, after a night of solitary prayer and communion with his soul, led Stonewall Jackson to march his VMI cadets out to join the Confederacy. Well, you know us rednecks. Iggorant cusses we is. The Great Man Himself has pronounced me tainted with that mystic belief in destiny which led Columbus and his mariners of 1492 to celebrate a final mass in the still-standing church at Palos, before they set sail from Spain on the voyage which gave this continent to our people.

I can hear the amateur racial pundits now: "Bah, Eye-ties and spics ain't proper Nordics anyway. Everbuddy knows people whose names end in vowels ain't White nohow. Iggorant Christian greaseballs! Now thim Viking fellers with the horns on their hats, they wuz proper pagan White men!" Ah, yes. Fine Nordic warrior heroes like Eric the Red, Leif Ericson, King Magnus, Harold Fairhair, Harald Hardrada and Erik Glipping, swilling their mead from drinking horns with a broadsword in one hand and a buxom blond maiden in other while they shouted to Odin!

I hate to break the news to some of these amateur racial theorists and half-assed historians, but all of the aforementioned legendary Norsemen were Christians, at least technically in the sense that they had been either baptized at birth or chose to convert in adulthood to gain some political advantage or other. True, their Christianity sat very lightly on some of them, but Olaf of Norway and the half-Danish Edward the Martyr of England even became saints.

As it happens, no, I am not a Christian in any recognizable sense of the word. My personal theology contains a bit of Identity, a bit of Nordic pagan mysticism, a *soupçon* of occultism, a dollop of Zen, a pinch of Swedenborg, and quite a few ideas so bizarre I don't discuss them in public for fear of being hauled away to the cackle box by gents in white coats. But my religious weirdness does not blind me to the immense and pivotal role that Christianity has played in the development of Aryan civilization. I refuse to slander and belittle the theology which has given to the ages the magnificent Gothic cathedrals of Europe; the beauty and glory of countless Renaissance artists like Michelangelo and Da Vinci; the awesome poetry and sweep of the English language at its' height in the King James Bible; a cumulative legacy of music, art, architecture, philosophy, exploration and conquest unparalleled in the history of humanity.

Let me make it clear that I understand the non-Christian viewpoint, and I accept it without reservation as a legitimate part of our Movement's philosophical and spiritual heritage. The non-Christians have much to say in their critique of Christianity which is valid and very pertinent to the future of our race.

Let us examine the whole issue briefly. Essentially, the anti-Christian (as opposed to the non-Christian) argument goes something like this: the preachers of the established churches have betrayed the White race. They preach that the Jews are God's Chosen People. They preach love-thy-nigger. More and more of them advocate and practice sodomy. They kiss the ass of every trendy minority and every politically correct cause of the moment, then go out and cheat on their wives and bugger altar boys. They practice every kind of fraud to obtain money which they spend on luxurious lifestyles for themselves. They prey on the faith and the weakness of the spiritually vulnerable, women, the elderly, the poorly educated and working class. They use religion as an opiate to keep the White wage slaves docile and obedient to Washington. They are disgusting race traitors, lickspittle System lackeys like Billy Graham and Jerry Falwell and Pat Robertson who have sold their racial birthright for Jacob's mess of pottage.

No argument from the Scribe, folks. I agree with all of the above. Most of the dog-collar crowd are garbage who need to be publicly hanged from balconies like the mob in Florence did to their archbishop and some of his monks back in 1478. (This seems to be an issue for historical trivia.)

But we are speaking here of the established, organized, professional clergy and Christian denominations of the present day, not the same breed as the popes who preached fiery sermons demanding Crusade against the infidel, the inquisitors who burned Jews by job lots long before Janet Reno, or Anglican bishop Leonidas Polk, who laid aside his robes and his crozier to become a general in the Confederate Army. It is obvious to anyone with even a smattering of history that Christianity was at one time a faith eminently suited to the dynamic, expanding Aryan folk. That it is now a threat to us I do not dispute, but the threat lies not in the faith itself, but in the *people* who have seized control of it and made it an instrument of political correctness. This is a clear distinction which anyone can perceive if they are not blinded by mindless hate.

It is not my place to defend Christianity or to point out the innumerable ways in which what is preached from today's pulpits contradicts what is in the Bible. There are others far more willing and able and qualified to do that than I. My contention is that anti-Christian bigotry is a potentially lethal weakness which may yet prove to be our Trojan horse, as it nearly was in the Klassen case. The fact is that we have among our ranks a vociferous minority who seem obsessed with an almost pathological hatred of the Christian faith and everything to do with it, even to the exclusion of the racial issue and the central urgency of White survival. I have known otherwise intelligent and dedicated comrades who would quite literally work themselves up into a screaming, raving seizure cursing and reviling Christianity. They are quite beyond reason on the subject. Indeed, it's fair to state that many of these Bible-bashers would rather the present state of affairs continue and the White race become extinct than the victory be won and an Aryan state established by the hated Christians.

For over twenty years, the Movement has numbered among its' many ongoing scandals the presence of a Jewish cult leader who was certainly a pederast and 99.9% certainly a murderer as well. People have often asked me how Klassen "got away with it" for so long. The most obvious answer, of course, is that the White racial nationalist movement in America is completely devoid of any moral standards or anything remotely resembling internal discipline, and anyone can get away with pretty much anything they like so long as they don't annoy ZOG sufficiently to get themselves imprisoned or killed. But that's certainly not the whole answer, not by a long shot. Klassen got away with it because, with the unerring sense of his Semitic ancestors for the Aryan's weak spot, he spotted this widespread pattern of obsessional anti-Christian behavior among White racial nationalists, and he decided that would be his hook, his gimmick when he set up shop. Until Your Friend and Humble Narrator came along, one of Old Benny Buttfuck's most effective weapons to silence criticism or excessive curiosity about his murky past was to treat it all as religiously-motivated persecution, emanating from kosher conservative Christian tub-thumpers. To be honest, some of it was.

But serious doubters and critics of the Klassen *ménage péderastique* were also tarred with the Christian brush. And untold hundreds of potentially valuable White activists the world over were thus neutralized, rendered completely ineffective and even harmful to the cause they sincerely wanted to serve, because they were so blinded by their hatred of Christianity that they could not see *who* and *what* they had become involved with. For some, like Brian Kozel, Matt Hayhow, Jürgen White and Jürgen Grobelaar, it will be forever too late.

The Buttfuckian saga is only one example of how anti-Christian hatred can obsess us, blind us to reality, and render us ineffective and counterproductive. These people of sound racial instinct, who could have performed valuable service to the cause, ended up in a complete dead end, wasting their time distributing some of the most venomously offensive literature ever produced in the name of the White man. Can you *imagine* the reaction of your average Joe Six-Pack when he picked up a copy of *Racial Loyalty* some Skinhead kid threw on his lawn, and saw pictures of scantily-clad women being flogged and articles babbling on and on about the deviate sexual acts supposedly committed in the Bible? God, I used to cringe every time I got that damned rag! Even the texture of the paper felt squamous and greasy, like Old Benny B. himself.

For twenty years, Benny Klassen used our own internal weaknesses to perform one gigantic act of psychological and political sodomy on the Movement. The COTC corpses stacked up like cordwood and Benny finally fled into hiding; today the buzzards tear at the carcass of his "church". Yet incredibly, there are those who still refuse to listen to the truth, even though they know perfectly well that Klassen was a fraud. To admit it would be to give aid and comfort to the despised Christians.

Unreason is our enemy. If there is to be a chance at all of victory, we must keep our heads clear for the struggle and see things as they are, not as we might wish them to be. The undeniable fact is that the vast majority of White Americans profess to some kind of Christianity. They may not practice their religion except on holidays, they may secretly doubt its tenets, but they will not tolerate being bombarded with childish, puerile blasphemy by people who are obviously obsessed and irrational on the one subject to the exclusion of all else. The debate on religion and the spiritual future of Aryan man is one which must take place at some point in the future, to be sure, but it must take place *after* we assume state power and are in control of the media of communications, and *after* we begin the reconstruction of society from top to bottom. Premature, divisive debate on the topic creates dissension and an uncalled-for window of opportunity for enemy agents provocateur, and for loathsome things like Klassen.

As to our pre-revolutionary, public position on religion, we have an ideal out, in the policy our forefathers set down in the Constitution, freedom of religion and liberty of conscience. If it was good enough for Washington and Franklin and Jefferson, it's good enough for us.

The Struggle That Dare Not Speak Its Name

In the 1890s, the degenerate aristocrat Lord Alfred Douglas was Oscar Wilde's bugger boy. In one of his poems, Douglas referred to homosexuality as "the love that dare not speak its name." There is a topic which the Aryan racial nationalist movement similarly has for years discussed only in whispers; it is time we came out of the closet and openly discussed armed struggle.

This article is a general discussion of certain aspects of human and political dynamics. It does not advocate, urge or incite any individual or group to commit unlawful acts of violence against anyone. The theoretical nature of this article should be clear to any reader of normal intelligence. I furthermore strongly caution you to beware of any person or group who approaches you with some alleged plan for armed insurrection or premature illegality. Anyone who does so is either a dangerous idiot or else a police agent of some kind. If you fall for their line, then *you* are an idiot. It is an ironic truism that, to some degree, Federal agents provocateur provide the Movement with a grim form of natural selection whereby those who are too stupid to become genuine revolutionaries are weeded out.

Bear in mind the essential difference between *direct action* and the *stupid illegal act.* One is the act of a man, the other the act of an overgrown and not very bright boy. Direct action is an overt act which inflicts serious damage against the enemy through the loss of important personnel or resources; an act which improves the Movement's image as serious revolutionaries to be treated with the respect which comes from the capacity to use force successfully; which demoralizes and confuses the enemy and correspondingly strengthens the morale of the Movement and the White population as a whole. Finally, the most critical component of direct action is that the persons carrying it out *are not apprehended or*

17

punished by the forces of the state.

By contrast, the *stupid illegal act* is usually carried out spontaneously, with little or no prior planning, often under the influence of alcohol. It is directed against minor targets such as street niggers, individual faggots or race-mixers, etc. who are no real loss to the system, there being plenty more where they came from. Finally, the perpetrators are almost always immediately arrested and given crushing prison sentences, thus boosting the enemy's morale and bolstering the deterrent effect of the establishment's crumbling legal machinery, giving it a gloss of efficiency which it does not in fact possess. Any more ritual disclaimers we need to insert? Can we get on with it? Good.

Such as it is, the Aryan racial nationalist movement throughout the world since 1945 has been distinguished by one remarkable characteristic which separates it from every other revolutionary movement ever known: a reluctance verging on the racially suicidal to engage in armed military struggle against genocidal tyranny.

Genuine politics is about one thing: the acquisition and exercise of *power.* All else is political hobbyism, a luxury which the wealthy landed gentry of the eighteenth and nineteenth centuries who created liberal democracy could afford, but which a race on the verge of extinction cannot. Power, all power without exception, is in the final analysis founded on one basis: *armed force.* Religion, constitutions, civil laws, custom and all the various social institutions for reinforcing acceptable behavior (i.e., submission to authority) all have their place in a state's power structure, but without the ultimate sanction of the bayonet they are meaningless.

All state power, without exception, is initially acquired through armed force or through the imminent threat of armed force. Some revolutions are bloodier than others; the Bolsheviks slaughtered millions while the National Socialist German Workers' Party came to power in Germany after somewhat less than a thousand deaths in fourteen years of street fighting between the Party's paramilitary formations and the Communists. But all modern states, without exception, were originally brought into existence by men who fought for power with weapons in their hands.

18

Power becomes accessible to revolutionaries when the existing order loses two vital assets upon which the maintenance of any government depends. The first element I refer to is the (at least passive) *consent of the governed,* and the second is the *credible monopoly of armed force.* When the revolutionary movement has both the will and the capacity to commit effective acts of armed insurrection against the state, and to do so with impunity, meaning the perpetrators *are not caught or punished,* then the state has lost the credible monopoly of force which is the foundation of all political power. Persons other than those sanctioned by the state have appropriated the wellspring; they exercise power over the lives and destinies of others. The revolutionary movement begins to displace the state's apparatus by armed compulsion as well as by transferring the consent of the governed to itself through persuasion and propaganda.

Both persuasion and coercion are necessary to carry out a successful revolution. Neither element alone can succeed without the other. Revolutionaries without a political and propaganda arm are mere bandits, while all the propaganda, all the popular support and all the legal activity in the world are useless if the state can fall back on armed force to maintain itself and destroy opposition. A revolutionary movement without an effective armed wing is doomed to perpetual futility and eventual defeat. These formulations are by no means original with me; they are as old as statecraft itself. I simply happen to be the only White racial nationalist who is willing to discuss them in public. These truths are obvious from even the most cursory examination of human history. They are also obvious from reading today's headlines. It is a demonstrable historical fact: pursued with sufficient persistence, ruthlessness, military expertise and fearless disregard for the consequences, armed struggle eventually *works.*

Why, then, do the White males of the late twentieth century persistently refuse to utilize the gun, the basic tool of power which is understood and applied without hesitation by the most savage African tribal leader and the most corrupt and uncouth Latin American despot? As a side issue of some interest, why does our present Aryan leadership (again, such as it is) consistently refuse even to address this question, instead expending a good deal of time and effort orchestrating extensive campaigns of slander and vilification against those who do?

There are several immediately apparent reasons. As discreditable as it is, a good part of it is simple garden-variety physical cowardice, as well as fear on the part of the "leaders" that any boat-rocking militancy will draw heat and frighten the racist couch potatoes who provide the bulk of the present constellation of grouplets' mail-order funding, sending them scuttling for cover, their precious checkbooks snapped shut like oysters. There is also the incredible lack of practical political education and knowledge among what passes for Aryan leadership, the bulk of whom are politically and historically illiterate. Your average Ku Klux Klan "leader" has never cracked a proper history book in his life and probably thinks Machiavelli is a foreign sports car. To be sure, some prominent Movement figures, especially those involved in Revisionism, do have a high degree of specialized knowledge within certain very narrow fields, such as Constitutional esoterica or the Third Reich period in Germany. But while they may be able to wax abstruse on obscure points of common law which the Federal judiciary of today simply ignores, or they can rattle off the name of every SS division and every Jew who was ever involved in Marxism, by and large any in-depth historical scholarship and analysis is almost entirely lacking within the Movement.

But our reluctance to face up to the reality of armed struggle's pivotal role in social and political change goes beyond these immediately apparent causes. It reaches into the deep-rooted psychological malaise which has pervaded the entire White racial resistance movement throughout the Western world since 1945. This psychological and spiritual condition is difficult to quantify. The late Dr. Revilo Oliver once posed the famous question: "Have we, the men of the West, lost the will to live?" Down through the years I have often observed that the White man in America seems to be in the grip of a kind of collective death wish, a mysterious and inexplicable *will to failure.* I am by no means the first to notice this phenomenon. One of the best articles the late Bob Miles ever wrote was in the aftermath of the Fort Smith sedition trials of 1988, when he pointed out in his From the Mountain newsletter that the acquittals in that despicable charade, instead of heartening us and encouraging more activism, resulted in an avalanche of sullen defeatism, smears, carping and dog-in-the-manger petty bickering throughout the Movement. Bob pointed out something which is crucial to understanding why we have gotten virtually nowhere for the past two generations. Over and above the preponderance of outright fraudulent leadership who are in it for the money, the Movement has been controlled for years by elements who are deeply pessimistic, defeatist, lazy, lethargic and mired in profound depression over Aryan man's terrible present situation and our more terrible prospects for the future. We are an army of Eeyores.

It's difficult to assign a precise point where the rot set in; the murder of Commander Rockwell will do for a benchmark, but the fact remains that for almost three decades the bulk of the White right in North America has been led by men who are simply going through the motions.

To be sure, sometimes they have gone through the motions with a certain style and panache. Yet with one or two shining exceptions, such as the saga of the Order, the multifarious attempts at White resistance which have occurred over the past thirty years have always had a dark, sinister leitmotif underlying them; the acidly poisonous idea that *victory isn't really possible,* that the White man is essentially doomed to extinction through his own stupidity, and that the most any of us can really do is to draw the funeral ceremonies out as long as we can, before getting on with the business of dying. When this attitude is taken into consideration, the reluctance seriously to discuss, much less to adopt, the one operational strategy 100 percent guaranteed to catapult us into serious politics in double-quick time becomes comprehensible. Why risk one's life, health and liberty on what is essentially an interesting but ultimately futile hobby? For that is exactly how most so-called "leaders" among us regarding the whole exercise in which they are engaged.

There are, of course, a number of very practical objections to Aryan armed struggle at the moment; please don't think I'm unaware of them. In the first place, we lack anything even remotely resembling leadership sufficiently competent to wage a military campaign. Tom Metzger regularly
incites his Skinhead followers to acts of random violence with hysterical rhetoric about "Aryan warriors," but this is just self-destructive hooliganism,
not properly organized revolution. Usually the Skins who fall into this trap end up doing more damage to themselves and their friends than to the

21

enemy, which result may of course be the object of the whole exercise.

A second objection is the serious dearth of Aryan men in this country of sufficiently strong and durable makeup even to serve as cannon fodder. On the whole, American White males are as soft as butter, a fact clearly evinced by the increasing number of White women who choose non-White men or other women as sexual partners. I do not mean soft only in the sense of physical fitness, although to be sure the bulk of America's weak-willed, flabby and self-indulgent White male population can't even run up a staircase without huffing and puffing. But physical strength is a minor problem and the one most easily corrected with some willpower and some exercise. If physical strength were everything, the orang-outang would rule the world. I refer to *spiritual* and *moral* softness; the infantile and egotistical all-American demand for instant gratification of every whim; the attention span of a housefly which characterizes our present Beavis and Butthead generation; the deathly fear of even the slightest physical pain or discomfort; the deeply-ingrained, bone-idle laziness which keeps the posterior of the White American firmly planted in his armchair staring at the tube like a zombie.

Almost nowhere in contemporary White American males do we find the attributes of the political soldier: the alertness to one's surroundings which means survival in guerrilla warfare; the cool and steady hand that can pull a trigger at close range and watch the brains splatter or detonate a bomb without fumbling or hesitation; the mental agility necessary to stay one step ahead of the pursuing police and government troops; and above all the total, selfless dedication, the inflexible purpose, the iron self-discipline necessary to function under unbelievable pressure, to stand the unimaginable stress and to live the life of the modern-day urban guerrilla. During my twenty-five years in the Movement I have met a few White men with that kind of inflexible will, hardness, courage and integrity, but only a few.

Before we can even think about rebelling against the tyrant, we must produce a different kind of White man in this country. This is not beyond the realm of possibility. I do not, in fact, believe that we ourselves will have to perform this prodigious transmutation. I think ZOG is going to do it for us. Because, you see, oppression either breaks men or it makes them. The philosopher Nietzsche said, "That which does not destroy me makes me stronger." The Jews and their leftist allies have turned this country into a revolting, putrid swamp, but dangerous beasts breed in swamps. I think the Jews and the establishment have long suffered from the typical defect which the arrogance of power breeds: an overestimation of their ability to control events. By denying jobs and educational opportunities to young White males through racial quotas, by persecuting those who resist with "hate crime" laws and vile civil lawsuits, by shouting their derision and their hatred for everything White through their controlled media and subjecting the White male to an unending torrent of insult, abuse and vilification, the scum who run this society are sowing dragon's teeth.

Assuming that we are serious about the survival of our race (an assumption which at times does not seem justifiable, but we'll let that go for the moment,) precisely what alternatives to the armed struggle have been proposed in order to achieve our objective? It is time we examined those alternatives realistically.

Every effort at building an effective White resistance movement has foundered on this central rock of contradiction: When all is said and done, precisely **what the hell do we intend to do?** How are we going to break the Judaic stranglehold which at present grips every aspect of American life? How are we going to get rid of the hordes of Third World mud people who now infest the North American continent and whose numbers swell every year since the government has abandoned all pretense of immigration control? How will we implement the historic Fourteen Words of David Lane and secure the existence of our people and a future for White children?

Shall we win some big election victory and walk into power with our enemies bowing and scraping and strewing flowers before us? Surely, *surely* there remains no one in this Movement who is so stupid as to continue to believe that such a thing is possible? One wonders what planet such people have been living on for the past thirty years. For one thing, since the inception of the Clinton co-presidency the Democratic party has gone to the Federal courts in several serious attempts to un-do statewide elections (in New Jersey and Texas) where the results displeased them. We will doubtless see more of this kind of thing as the American political system continues its present downward slide into

Third World sleaze and degradation. And if the Democrats will pull this stunt with respectable Republican conservatives who were so rude as to win elections, what do you think would happen if an open National Socialist or Klansman were to win an elective office? The Democrats, the Republicans, the Anti-Defamation League of B'nai B'rith and Morris Dees would all go running to the nearest Federal judge as fast as their bandy little legs could carry them and get an injunction to prevent the White winner from taking office until some way could be found to overturn the election results.

I suppose there might be a few who continue to cite the example of David Duke, but Duke's subsequent career since his Louisiana state election victory in 1989 conclusively demonstrates the futility of racial nationalist participation in electoral politics. Duke ran for the U. S. Senate and for Governor; he lost both elections due to blatant vote fraud which was carried out by Louisiana state elections officials and tacitly condoned by the Federal Election Commission. Duke furthermore had to spend several years battling bogus legal charges over his campaign finances, charges he eventually won clear of but which bankrupted him. David Duke's 1989 victory was an **accident.** It won't be allowed to happen again.

Aside from the massive vote fraud which has become a regular feature of American elections, demographics increasingly dictate against our use of electoral politics. The simple fact of the matter is that White people in general are becoming outnumbered in large parts of this country, and racially conscious White people even more so. The various Third World minorities, the left-wing, union, feminist and faggot bloc votes will combine with that solid lump of White jackasses who simply will not change their voting patterns no matter how much it would be in their racial interest to do so. And suppose we *did* win a few minor public offices? Elected officials in this society no longer wield much in the way of effective power. True power is concentrated unconstitutionally in the hands of the Federal judiciary and the massive civil service bureaucracy. There is little point in getting our people elected to talking shops whose primary function in these times is to rubber-stamp the power structure's true agenda.

Communalism, then? The formation of Aryan communities or

colonies or whatever, far out in the deep forests of the Ozarks or the Pacific Northwest? We saw on Ruby Ridge and in Waco what ZOG has planned for separatists of any racial or religious stripe who attempt to unplug themselves from the tube and who refuse to function as mere economic units of production and consumption within the New World Order.

So what should we do? For the time being we must stick with legality *as a tactic of convenience and expediency only,* which is all legality ever is for any truly revolutionary movement. But we need to accept that the entire thrust of the Movement from this point on must be aimed at *preparation for eventual armed struggle* in order to seize state power and create a genuine New Order, a new way of life in America. At some point in the future, the White man in North America will be confronted with a choice: He must either fight for his right to exist here, literally, in the sense of armed combat with military weapons, or he must perish and hand his children over into slavery. We cannot save our people if we persistently refuse even to discuss physical resistance against the government which is enslaving us and the anthropoid sub-species who butcher us like hogs for sport. We cannot hope to lead our children out of the terrible world into which they have been born if we lie to them and lie to ourselves that ultimate salvation will be found in a ballot box or a computer terminal behind which we can sit on a soft cushioned chair. If our race is to survive then there must come a time of blood, death, and fire.

Finally, we will inevitably hear the last quavering objections of the Nervous Nellies who wail and bleat, "But it's the law! We can't break the precious, wonderful, sacred *laaaaw* of *Amurrrrrrica!"*

Well, they're quite right. Bill and Hillary *are* the law. Tyrants always are. That's what distinguishes tyrants from ordinary gangsters. Stalin was the law in Russia, too. Integration is the law. Affirmative action is the law. Quotas in university admissions are the law. Every April 15th the law robs you of one-third of what you earn all year. Drugs and black crime and the Third World hordes swarming over the borders are ignored by the law. Any little light bulbs coming on over your head yet?

The law is a weapon, and like any other weapon it is only as good or as bad as the people wielding it. Right now the law is in the hands of the present United States government and the liberal establishment, one of many such weapons. It is being used to pillage you, disrupt and break up your family, rob your children of a future, and will eventually destroy you in your old age. The law in its present state deserves no respect from any White man or woman in America. Indeed, obedience and respect for the law have become countersurvival and, human nature being what it is, anything which is countersurvival will not endure. Adolf Hitler himself stated in *Mein Kampf:* "When a people is being driven to destruction through the instrument of governmental authority, then rebellion is not only the right, but the duty of that people." This point is so obvious that I really can't make it any more clear; if you honestly don't understand this, then you should not be in the Movement at all.

Finally, there is the moral dimension to be considered. Looking for easy outs and safe shortcuts is not only futile, it is wrong. Before we can have a new White world, we must *earn* it. That's the way life works.

Like all persecuted minorities, White males are despised. We are despised by the government, by the liberal establishment, by the congoid criminals who rob and rape and kill our people, by the media, and to a large degree we are despised by our own children. We are despised because we are correctly viewed as weak, cowardly, lazy, incapable and unwilling to defend ourselves or take any serious action against those who despoil and victimize us, other than to go whining to the enemy's police and the enemy's courts. Why in the name of God *should* anyone respect us? Why should we respect ourselves?

It's time that White men recovered our self-respect and the respect of those who hate us. And it is a longstanding human truth that respect among men is earned by the shedding of blood.

America's Peasants

One of my hobbies is medieval history. Some years ago I was reading a scholarly volume on the Middle Ages when I came across a translation of a textbook or primer used to teach children of the nobility to read, kind of a fourteenth-century "See Dick And Jane" kind of thing. The book described all the various people who existed in the medieval world and their functions: the king rules by divine right, the baron gives justice and protection to his people, the knight does deeds of valor for his lady love, the priest intercedes with God for the souls of men, the merchant brings goodies from foreign lands. It continued on down to the tradesmen such as the weavers, the butchers and bakers and so forth, you get the picture. At the very end was a single sentence thrown in almost as an afterthought which described people who in those days were at least 90% of the entire population. It was a phrase which has stuck in my mind from that day to this: *"And the peasant works so that all may eat."*

I can think of no better way to describe the role of the White man today, and many White women excluding the artificial affirmative action created female managerial class. We are peasants. Our function in this society is simple. The peasant labors so that all may eat. White men build and drive the trucks that deliver the consumer goods, manufacture and package the junk food, maintain the power plants that keep the air conditioners and televisions running, cut down the trees and make the paper which keeps the bureaucracy going. White police and soldiers loyally carry the guns and pull the triggers for ZOG, everywhere in the world. Above all, White men pay the overwhelming bulk of the taxes which keep the whole rotten system afloat. We are serfs on the great worldwide consumer plantation, producing the wealth and keeping everything going while our multifarious masters sit on the veranda eating and drinking the products of our labor and spinning their pointless little

27

intrigues. Like all peasants, we have no place in the political process. Our role is to work so that all may eat, accept with gratitude such consumer goodies as our betters see fit to fill our bowls with, shuffle, tap dance, tug the forelock, vote the way we are told to vote by our natural superiors the liberals, and apply our lips in the prescribed manner to whatever derrières are presented to us. Finally, we must keep our minds squeaky clean of any impure doubt or racist thought.

But peasants have been known to revolt. Think guillotine, my brothers, with a pile of heads on the Capitol steps higher than Tamerlane's. Think gallows on the White House lawn, with rows of bodies in thousand dollar suits with pedicured toes turning slowly in the wind. The French did it. The Russians did it. The Germans did it. Even the Iraqis and Iranians did it. So will we.

Some Seasonal Good Cheer

There are times when it seems beyond doubt that we are living in the age of the triumph of evil. Believe it or not, there is still some good in the world. Not much, and on the rare occasions when it shows itself, goodness must peep up from its hiding place like a cautious groundhog, then pop back underground very quickly to avoid the swooping predators. But every now and then we get a glimpse.

Kameraden

On October 31st Herbert Perry, a retired businessman in Durham, North Carolina suffered a stroke. He recovered in hospital and early in November was sent to Hillcrest Convalescent Home. He had a roommate, an 88 year-old man named Helmut Bartsch, who had been on a visit from Germany to his married daughter in Durham and who had also suffered a stroke on October 25th.

At first the two elderly gentlemen didn't talk much, but then Perry's son-in-law brought him some of his effects from home, including a bedside clock with a B-17 bomber on top. It turned out the two roomies had something in common. "Ah, I remember that silhouette," spoke up Bartsch when he saw it. "I remember the sound, too. It was like a hammer of smiths, crack, crack, crack."

Over 50 years ago, Herbert Perry was a corporal in the Army Air Corps in England, an air traffic controller. Helmut Bartsch was across the Channel in Normandy, commanding an anti-aircraft battery in the Wehrmacht. "I put 'em up, he shot 'em down," commented Perry to a local news reporter. "We're very similar even though we're enemies," continued Perry. "He had a stroke on the right side, I had a stroke on the

29

left side. Now we talk about our days in the army. Every time he gets a little blue we sing a German hymn."

"The newspapers were always reporting American air attacks on small towns," said Bartsch, explaining why he volunteered for anti-aircraft duty. "It was my duty to serve in the army." Herbert Perry lost a lot of friends among the air crews he sent up into the sky, heading for Germany, many of them never to return, but he never let himself become bitter and he has always maintained a deep respect for the German people and their culture and intellect. "I even said it back during the war. The German people were smart and if the Americans hadn't come to England Hitler would have conquered them." The two families are now friends and the old vets will be staying in touch after Bartsch returns to Stuttgart.

Better Late Than Never

Crawford J. Ferguson of Charlotte, North Carolina is 72 years old. Half a century ago Ferguson was part of a B-17 crew that flew 35 missions over Germany in 1944, raids which slaughtered untold hundreds of thousands of people. For fifty years it has haunted his sleep. "I keep seeing the plumes of fire down below as the cities fall apart, and at the same time it's like I'm down in the city, burning, running through the flames looking for a child or a wife or a sister," Ferguson told a reporter. "I have known for years that there was something I had to do before I die."

What Ferguson had to do was apologize, and this year he did so. He wrote out a total of 13 letters, about 100 words each, and addressed them to the city hall in every German town his plane had ever bombed: Berlin, Bremen, Cologne, Frankfurt, Kassel, Hamburg, Munich, and others not revealed in the news article. In each letter he put a simple, heartfelt apology for what he had done in 1944. "Our target was strategic, but innocent lives were lost, citizens maimed and civilian property destroyed. I beg forgiveness for the agony I helped inflict upon you..." The first few letters got some publicity in Germany; the mayor of Kassel sent Ferguson a thank-you note and the local newspaper printed the apology. A weekly TV news program called "Hessenschau" picked up the story and ran a feature on it. Ferguson also received a letter from the Munich city council, requesting permission to make his letter public, which he granted. The mayor of Munich, Christian Ude, wrote a personal letter of thanks.

Then something odd happened. About half of Ferguson's letters got through, but six of them appear to have been intercepted and returned by the German Federal postal authorities without explanation, possibly because they were deemed to contain "Nazi propaganda". Ferguson says with wry humor, "I wrote to our beloved President Bill Clinton. I sent the letters to him and I told him they had been returned. I invited him to read them and if he thought they merited being forwarded I was going to rely on him to take care of the situation. I've still not heard back from him."

"He Is One Of Us Now."

I read this in a British newspaper over ten years ago, and I can't remember all the details; I will quote from memory as best I can.

In a small village in the Norfolk fen country is a war memorial cemetery for the local dead in both wars. In one corner stands a small white obelisk bearing a Luftwaffe eagle and Swastika. In the early 1980s some of the "anti-fascist" scum came up from London to squawk and deface and attempt to destroy the headstone. The police and a number of local men came to the cemetery and saw them off, apparently none too gently. The "antifas" scurried back to London screaming about police brutality and right-wing vigilantes. In the course of reporting this, the press also retold how the stone came to be there.

In 1944 and 1945 a lot of British and American air groups were operating out of small airfields all across East Anglia. One such was this place in Norfolk. One day there was a massive daylight raid against what was left of Hamburg, using planes from all over these various fields. They dropped their load of death and were headed home when they ran into a number of German fighters. "We broke up and flew our separate ways back to base, but there was this one German who stuck with us and wouldn't give up," recalled an American pilot. "He shot down at least two planes in our group and probably some more when the dogfight first

31

began, but we just couldn't shake him. Our radio operator spoke some German and he could hear this guy's flight commander ordering him to come back, he would run out of fuel if he didn't, but the German pilot told him something like, 'You saw what they did today. They left nothing. I have nothing to go back to.' Evidently we'd bombed this guy's house, probably killed his family.

"We dodged into a cloud formation and for a while we thought we'd lost him, but over the coast of Holland we had to drop down and get our bearings, and there he was, still on our tail, still shooting at us, shredding us up pretty bad and wounding two of our crew. Our own gunners shot back but could never hit him. Damn if the SOB didn't chase us all the way back to England! Our flak opened up on him as we came over the English coast, but they missed. By the time we got back to our field he had two British Spitfires on his tail, but they couldn't seem to tag him either. The guy seemed bulletproof. I got her down and we all jumped out of the aircraft and ran like hell, dragging our wounded with us, and he crashed his Messerschmitt right into our B-17. He finally got us, even though it was at the cost of his own life. His plane didn't catch fire because his fuel tanks were bone dry; he must have been flying on fumes. When they pulled him out of the wreckage dead we saw this blond kid, couldn't have been more than 19 or 20. He didn't have any papers on him, and we never learned his name." The incident had been witnessed by the villagers, who were so impressed by the boy's courage that the local vicar offered him a burial plot in the churchyard, where he lies to this day, unknown.

All of the above is quoted from memory, but one thing I do remember with absolute accuracy, because I wrote them down, and that is the words on that young hero's grave in an enemy land. They were composed by an RAF colonel who also witnessed his death: *"Call them misguided, call them even wicked if you must; but no nation or cause ever brought forth defenders of greater courage and worth. They fought like the Northland gods of their ancient and warlike race, and few indeed are those among us who can say that ever we saw their backs."*

When the British media asked the local people why they defended the grave of a Nazi, one of them answered, "We don't care what he was. We just know that he was a brave lad who one morning flew all the way from Germany to our village to die here, because he thought it was right that he do so. He is one of us now, and when those yobs came up here from London and insulted his memory they insulted us and all our own dead as well. They weren't even alive during the war, they don't know what it was like back then. Why don't they just bloody well belt up?"

* * *

These are the words of the men who were there, who fought the Jews' war for them, and who are far more entitled to speak of that time and those other men than any Deborah Lipstadt, or anile Ken McVay, or slobbering Rich Graves. I have met many such down through the years who were veterans of that war, and I never pass up a chance to see if I can get them to speak of their experiences. While I have to concede that there is a great deal of hatred remaining among those who fought against the Japanese, I have never met a single genuine combat veteran of any Allied army, be they American, Canadian, British or South African, who actually fought against the Germans, who did not speak with respect and admiration of their courage, their skill and devotion as soldiers, and their human qualities of fortitude, humor and compassion in victory and in defeat. If there are those who can't handle this view of the Nazis, then I recommend you start with some of the accounts left by Allied veterans of the first war. (Robert Graves' *Goodbye To All That* springs to mind, but there are many other good examples.)

As for these hate-filled reptiles at the Simon Wiesenthal Center and the ADL and the AFA and Nizkor, I can only quote again the little old English lady: "Why don't they just bloody well belt up?"

Why indeed?

[January 1997]

What Is The New World Order?

Alternative political people all across the spectrum tend to bandy the term New World Order around quite a bit, generally as a designation for the government or the Jews or the Trilaterals or the multinational banks or just "them". The NWO is all these things, but it is not just a collection of institutions and people, it is an idea, a genuine (if thoroughly evil) vision of mankind's future. The best way I've ever heard it put is that it's the idea of the great global consumer plantation, a social and economic order ruled by a tiny and immensely wealthy Anglo-Zionist elite who will command a worldwide population of homogenous, coffee-colored industrial serfs bred from the forced admixture of all the present races of the earth. Another way to describe the NWO would be the final development of capitalism.

For several centuries, first Europe and then the rest of the world have been torn between two conflicting philosophies, both of them Jewish in origin. Capitalism arose from the collapse of the feudal system and the infiltration of Jewish bankers and moneylenders into the European economy during the Renaissance. The more recent Marxism is of course named after the rabbi's son of Trier, Karl Marx, but its tenets are actually of older and of somewhat obscure origin. You've got your Levelers and whatnot from the seventeenth century, and of course the Adam Weishaupt episode from the eighteenth. I've never completely bought the entire Illuminati story, but there were very definite Marxist elements in the French Revolution, Hébert and his lot, etc.

This isn't the time or the place to go into a long digression on the history and ideology of these two competing forces, but basically both Marxism and capitalism share the same materialistic, essentially Judaic view of mankind and the human condition. Both consider man to be an *economic animal,* and see human beings as interchangeable units of economic production and consumption. People are merely components of

34

the great economic machine either of "the marketplace" or the "dictatorship of the proletariat". They are human animals who have only material needs which must be met at a certain minimal level in order to keep them functioning in the economy. People have no spiritual needs or identity, no culture, no race, no religion, no aspirations, no independent thought. They exist solely to be installed like spare parts and worked until they are broken or worn out, when the system then pulls them out, throws them away, and installs a replacement part.

It is essential to understand this opinion of people by both capitalism and Marxism, because it is this view of man as a soulless, raceless component in a human anthill which has led to the imposition of the thoroughly bogus idea of racial equality in both capitalist and socialist countries. Both systems are instinctively aware of the fact that their ideology is incorrect, that men are *not* soulless economic units whose sole purpose in life is to work and to consume and generate profits for the elite. But instead of accepting Nature's human creation and changing their ideology (thus giving up their profits and elite status), both Marxism and capitalism seek to *change mankind* into the coffee-colored, mindless, cultureless mass of docile workers their philosophies envision. This is why both Marxism and capitalism are evil: by seeking to recreate mankind to fit their own ideas of what men and women should be, they are challenging God. Like two demented moral Frankensteins, Marxism and capitalism have both decided they can do a better job than the Creator.

It is now apparent that Marxism *per se* has lost the contest, but capitalism has by now absorbed a number of welfare-statist aspects of Marxism and so what we have is now a kind of meld between the two, although there are some signs that capitalism is reverting to its older nineteenth-century *laissez-faire* form and by the next century if unchecked may have eliminated all of the aspects of Marxism it assimilated during the time of competition. In any case, capitalism is now moving full speed ahead to seize control of the entire planet and its resources, and to create the pliable brown workforce it requires to create the global plantation for the generation of obscene profits the like of which the world has never seen before. This effort is, of course, spearheaded by the United States and behind the U. S. the world corporate power structure.

We see evidence of this in the growing tendency towards military

35

intervention around the world, actually a form of piecemeal conquest; the blue-helmeted troops come to "bring peace" and somehow they never seem to leave. We see this in the virtual abandonment of any form of immigration control in North America and throughout Europe; White countries are being flooded with Third World mud and already we can see published references in the controlled media to "eliminating racism by eliminating race", i.e. mass compulsory interbreeding. We see this in the forced unification of Europe; in NAFTA and GATT; in the looting of Russia and the Eastern European countries by corporate buccaneers; in...well, you get the picture. It's all around us. You'll find that when you study the news from this viewpoint, all of a sudden things start making sense. The role of the Jews in all of this should not be ignored, but neither should it be overstated. They are a significant part of the problem, but not the whole problem. (The problem essentially lies in the inner spiritual weakness and confusion of White men throughout the world; once the White man changes his thinking and recovers his ancient courage our victory is certain.)

For Aryan man there is only one alternative. We were shown the way by the Third Reich and by the German nation who for twelve glorious years refused to act like rats in a maze knocking themselves out for a bit of cheese. In 1933 the Germans "broke the plantation", and it took the entire world to force them back on again. But times are different now, and the New World Order is in fact far weaker and more disorganized, more corrupt and more confused and less able to suppress rebellion than it was in 1939. National Socialism survives even in Germany, despite the most vicious persecution. Like Marxism, unrestrained capitalism *doesn't work,* although it does function more effectively, but for a time only. Eventually capitalism's contradictions catch up with it. The New World Order is already starting to fumble. If you will pardon me a final paraphrase from an old Marxist propaganda saw, you may think we National Socialists are beating our heads against a wall. So we are—but it's a rotten wall, and a few good kicks will send it crashing down into the dust.

[February 1997]

Our Socialism

This week, I am going to be talking about something which seems to cause a lot of concern and curiosity, and that is why we use the term socialism in our Party's name and in the name of our world view, National Socialism. To tell the truth, we don't get anywhere nearly as much concern about our use of the word today as we used to get many years ago when there were more conservative elements in the Movement, but it still happens. There are still a few people to whom the very word socialism conjures up visions of the Kremlin and they simply can't get around that idea, even though it is completely incorrect. The result is that we still occasionally get people who jump up and call us Communists because of that word socialism. But there is a very definite reason why we have that second word as part of our name.

The first thing I want to explain to you is that there are many different kinds of socialism. You are probably most familiar with the kind known as Communism, as originally formulated in the middle of the nineteenth century by the Jew Karl Marx, but there are several other kinds. There is the mild Social Democratic version, what we here in America call liberalism. The principles are the same; basically, liberals are really Marxists without the courage of their convictions. You might say that liberals are decaffeinated Marxists. Then there are all the various weird ultra-left versions of Marxism like those practiced in North Korea, Communist China, Peru, etc. Most kinds of so-called socialist philosophies are in fact some variation of Marxism. This is where National Socialism differs from all the rest, because our socialism is not based on the writings of the Jew Marx, but on the character of our Aryan race.

Marxist Socialism or Communism is in essence the flip side of the coin of capitalism, which I have discussed earlier on this series. Like

37

capitalism, Marxism holds that man is essentially an economic unit of production and consumption, a cog in the wheel of a great machine which needs to be fed and lubricated and maintained and then thrown away when he can no longer perform his allotted function. Yes, I know I have said this before, and possibly some of you are getting bored with it, but I'm going to keep on repeating it, because there is no more important lesson for you to learn regarding the nature of today's. Our struggle is largely one of spirituality and idealism against materialism, and the two forces which have shaped the twentieth century and which still pretty much control our destiny even today, Communism and capitalism, are both profoundly *materialistic* philosophies. This is where National Socialism differs so greatly from both of them; **National Socialism is based on Man, while the others are based on Matter.**

At any rate, to get back to the central topic, our socialism is not materialistic or economic. It is based on the now almost obsolete concept of *social duty,* the idea that no man is an island and that along with rights and privileges we all have duties and obligations to our communities and to the culture and people into which we were born. This idea used to be commonly accepted to the point where no one questioned it; now it has virtually disappeared from our national life. Our socialism teaches that there is something more important in life than the frantic pursuit of little green pieces of paper and the temporary security and pleasure these little pieces of paper can bring. Our socialism is the socialism of the man who doesn't just sit and watch while his neighbor's house is on fire, he helps to put the fire out.

We are in the terrible situation we are in today very largely because we have decided that each of us can go our own way and to hell with everybody else. White people have decided voluntarily to strip ourselves of our racial and cultural identity because it interferes with making money. In doing so we become exactly what the capitalist system wants us to be, economic units of production and consumption, and nothing more. But we are not born as faceless, raceless, cultureless beings who are only good for working and buying things at the mall. Race and spirituality are *genetic,* they are in our blood, and those qualities are in themselves a kind of socialism, because they form a bond between all peoples of the Aryan race. Our socialism is first of all a kind of sense of

38

community which people in healthy Aryan societies always have demonstrated.

Secondly, there is a difference between *big* government as defined by the liberals and the Red socialists, i.e. what we have now in this country, and *responsible* governments. While National Socialists do not believe in a cradle to grave welfare state and while we support free enterprise, we do understand and believe that the state has certain moral and economic and political obligations to its citizens.

Never fall into the trap of so-called libertarianism. Libertarianism is basically just a moral front for the worst kind of *laissez-faire*, 19th-century style buccaneer monopoly capitalism. Libertarians have this idea that the state needs to be kept as weak and as completely close to non-existent as possible, and for that some people call them anarchists, which they are not. They are capitalists. I think most libertarians know perfectly well what would happen if the state were to wither away or disappear; we wouldn't have freedom, what we would have would be the large multi-national corporations stepping in to fill the gap. So let's trash can this libertarian idea that the state is always bad; that depends entirely on who is controlling the state and what purpose the machinery of the state is being put to. In an Aryan society the state does have duties and obligations to the Aryan folk which go beyond maintaining and army and a post office. The state has the obligation to ensure that everyone has the right to a job and the right to earn his living and support his family in peace and security. Furthermore, the state has a duty to make sure that jobs exist; that the common economy is being run sufficiently well and competently to produce employment and prosperity. The state has the obligation to ensure that no citizen is denied necessary medical care because of lack of money. The state has the obligation to ensure that every one of its citizen has a decent and affordable place to live. The state has the obligation to ensure that Aryan children have a clean and safe and livable environment in which to grow up. The state has an obligation to ensure that no Aryan suffers in their old age from cold or hunger or deprivation.

There is nothing wrong with these duties or with using tax money to implement them, so long as they are done by and for *White people*. You need to understand that like everything else on the continent of North

America, so-called welfare dependency and socialistic policies are a *racial* issue. Always remember that *everything in America comes down to race.* Present-day welfare dependency is a problem because recipients of all these welfare payments and scams are overwhelmingly black or else, increasingly, mud-colored Third World immigrants.

The abuses of the welfare state are carried out almost entirely by blacks and Third Worlders. In the social services area, like every other aspect of American life, the vast improvements which would be achieved by removing blacks and other non-Whites from our society really boggle the mind when you sit down and think about them. As to the welfare-dependency mentality which occasionally appears among White people, especially in Europe, this would disappear once these people living in council estates and whatnot were shown that they have a stake in society once again, that the state was being run by White people, for White people, for the common good of the race and nation and not just as a grab bag of goodies to be given away to everybody with a black or a brown skin. Sure, some White people have developed a bad attitude towards welfare and food stamps. They look around and they see blacks and Mexicans and Cambodians and Filipinos and God knows what all else getting all this loot from the government and they take the attitude,. "Hey, why shouldn't I get some?" That's not the best attitude in the world, but it's understandable.

In National Socialist Germany, after the revolution of 193 3, not one single Aryan child went hungry, not a single German family went without a home, not a single German worker was unemployed within a year or so after the triumph of the Führer and the NSDAP. The whole nation pitched in with Winter Relief programs and things like one-pot meals twice a week, until the economy was fixed and Germany went back to work. Marxist labor unions were abolished and a genuine Labor Front was established to represent all German workers, established so successfully that right up until 1945 German industry was still in full production for the war effort and invading Allied troops found factory lines still turning out supplies and munitions. Efforts like that are not made by disgruntled or oppressed workers. An entire social services structure was erected in order to support the German family and bring order and peace and tranquility to German society, and right up until 1945, it worked. A

40

Reichs Labor Service was created which built the mighty autobahns which are still used today and who reclaimed millions of acres of arable agricultural land from swamps and from the sea to feed the German people. Medical facilities and child care in Nazi Germany was the best in the world for its time. Social problems like divorce, alcoholism, and homosexuality virtually disappeared. That is true socialism in action.

Not Known, But Knowable

Timothy McVeigh has been betrayed. He has been betrayed by his own attorney. He has been betrayed by the former associates who were involved in the Oklahoma City bombing with him. He has been betrayed by the Federal government of the United States who set up the whole incident as a sting operation in order to rehabilitate the discredited BATF and to get the draconian Clinton "anti-terrorist" legislation passed and thus introduce gun confiscation and prior-restraint censorship of political speech into the United States.

People have asked me what I think of Order Judge Richard Matsch's refusal to allow BATF informant Carol Howe to testify. That gets into the whole Dennis Mahon-Andreas Strassmeir thing. I admit I am having to somewhat re-assess my views on the matter. The sudden convenient indictment of Carol Howe is very suspicious indeed; according to media reports there doesn't seem to be a shred of actual evidence against either her or her current live-in toy boy. It is difficult to believe that she was not indicted to get a handle on her and destroy her credibility as a witness. The idea that Dennis Mahon was involved in anything like this is simply stupid to anyone who knows him, as I do. I have had an opportunity to speak with two people who knew Andreas Strassmeir well, and one assures me that "Andy" was "kind of like a German Gilligan", i.e. a bumbling nonentity who never tried to get any information or start any trouble and for some odd reason seemed interested only in military models and dating American women. The other swears to me that Strassmeir "acted too stupid to be stupid", but this may be 20/20 hindsight combined with right-wing paranoia. This source also claims that Strassmeir was constantly talking about guns, bombs, and violence, the mark of the provocateur.

I find it somewhat understandable that the government would target the harmless Elohim City commune for this kind of sting; ever since Waco the regime and their Hollywood lap dogs have been striving mightily to "prove" that any group of people who choose to separate themselves from the rat race and the boob toob and go off and live their own way by themselves are violent maniacs who must be put in prison by the valiant BATF. But on the balance, I still think the Strassmeir-Mahon scenario is a crock, not only because there is a complete lack of anything resembling evidence with the exception of a BATF informer slut, but because of the people who have been pushing the Strassmeir-Mahon scenario for all its worth.

Specifically I am very mistrustful of a so-called "militia magazine" called *John Doe Times* which suddenly appeared on the internet and which is devoted entirely to trying to blame OKC on "neo-Nazis"; this is put out by a so-called militia group which seems to have no existence of any kind outside the internet, and is written by what appears to me to be an intelligent and articulate person who is *trying* to write and act like a semi-literate redneck. I am also deeply suspicious of anything which comes from the mysterious and highly dubious "free lance journalist" going under the name of J. D. Cash. According to media reports this man was apparently involved with defense lawyers in an abortive attempt to frame Louis Beam for the bombing. It was "Cash" who came up with Carol Howe and started this whole ridiculous Strassmeir business, which attempts to rope in not only Mahon and Beam and Elohim City but crusading attorney Kirk Lyons who just happened (surprise, surprise!) to be handling the Waco wrongful death suits. As far as I am concerned, "Cash" blew his cover by trying to kill too many birds with the OKC stone.

Beyond this I have a problem. As most of you are aware, I believe I know at least part of the secret of Oklahoma City. I am, however, under a court injunction which effectively orders me not to publish anything about Oklahoma City which does not conform to the officially sanctioned parameters of speculation on the subject. If this injunction came from any other source than the one it does, I would be in court with bells on tomorrow, an American Civil Liberties lawyer in tow, challenging this completely unconstitutional assault on my civil rights. However, it has become quite clear over the past few months that a large part of the overall objective of the people who are involved in this grotesque episode (and there are many more than just one), is to degrade and discredit the entire Aryan racial nationalist movement by creating a public spectacle which will make anyone who holds racial views of any kind into a figure of fun as we throw mud at one another. It is becoming increasingly obvious *whose interests are being served* in this matter, and I am happy to say that the penny finally seems to be dropping within the Movement that these people are not who and what they say they are, and have not been for some time. However, that does not help me in the short run as regards publishing the truth about Oklahoma City.

For the time being I have decided not to touch this particular tar baby. If I thought my knowledge might affect the outcome of events it would be a different story, but by now it's pretty clear that we are looking at a JFK assassination-level cover-up here and anything I say would simply be ignored, as it has been, indeed, by the media and by McVeigh's defense team. This problem will not last forever, and there are ways and means by which the truth can and will be made known. Until then, my views on the matter may be summed up as follows: the truth about Oklahoma City is not known—but it is knowable.

How *Not* To Do It

Our Movement has one great talent: we are absolute aces at demonstrating how *not* to go about resisting tyranny and genocide.

That statement is only about half sarcastic; negative lessons can be of benefit *if we can learn from them* an ability we don't seem to be able to develop. The latest is that some "American militia group" has been busted in Canada, of all places, "training" out in the north woods somewhere, with (of course) an arsenal of weapons which has now been confiscated. Depending on the degree of corruption in the RCMP or provincial police units involved, the guns will either be destroyed or sold on the black market to criminals. Certain it is that not one single round from any of those weapons will ever be fired at the racial enemy. I don't know many further details, but I don't need to. We've all heard the story before.

Look, I know none of you militia or survivalist types or Order wannabes out there are going to listen to me. I have come to accept down through the years that the gods have afflicted me with the Curse of Cassandra; I speak the truth and it goes in one ear and out the other. Nonetheless, it is my duty to speak on. I am going to tell you some things about guerrilla warfare. I am far more entitled to speak on this subject that 90% of you. I have served in two armies and two wars, and I have lived in three countries, (Rhodesia, South Africa, and Ireland) which were undergoing guerrilla insurgency, plus I study history and politics and revolutionary movements as a lifelong vocation. Acting on the highly tenuous proposition that you guys are serious if muddled in your intentions and are not simply acting out middle-aged Rambo fantasies, I am going to give you a few pointers on how *not* to wage an insurrection against a powerful and entrenched regime.

Now, do I need to stick in the usual ritual disclaimers here, in order to advise you what *not* to do? Hmmm...probably not. Okay, let's push the envelope a bit. This time I won't bother with the multifarious semantic fig leaves we generally use to try and pretend that we're not really saying what we're saying. It doesn't fool anyone anyway, and I rather doubt any of these disclaimers would make a dime's worth of difference in a Zionist court. Now attend, my children:

1. Revolutionary movements do not have post office boxes.

They do not have newsletters. They do not have web pages. They do not solicit donations in the mail from right-wing mailing lists. They do not maintain mailing lists themselves or keep any written records of any kind for the enemy to seize.

2. Revolutionary movements *act.* They do not *talk.*

I am presently fighting my own fight with words. I do not pretend otherwise. If I felt that armed revolt was appropriate for the place and time and for me personally then I would not be talking, I would be shooting. I would *not* be talking about how I was going to start shooting just any old time now when the spirit moved me. Nor would I be sending people threats in the mail or leaving threatening messages on their answering machines and getting myself a lengthy prison sentence. This is the act of an idiot. Threatening someone at all is the act of an idiot. If you genuinely mean to carry out your threat then you are simply putting your target on his guard. If you don't mean to carry out your threat then you are a coward and a disgrace to the cause you purport to serve who makes us all look ridiculous. A large part of the lack of respect our point of view commands in this country is due to the fact that so many of our people are quite obviously pompous blowhards who dress up in camouflage uniforms and wave their semi-autos in the air for the television cameras talking and bragging about all the valiant deeds they're going to do at some unspecified time down the pike. You might call this the Terre Blanche syndrome. We lost a whole country like that, South Africa. Please, *please,* PLEASE don't make fools of yourself and fools of the rest of us by doing this.

There's an old saying, "Don't talk the talk if you're not going to walk the walk." I disagree. Don't talk the talk at all, under any circumstances. Either *do it* and then *keep your mouth shut* both before and after—or just plain keep your mouth shut.

3. Do not stockpile weapons. Do not stockpile explosives. Do not stockpile anything at all.

Stockpiles are nothing but juicy propaganda plums for the BATF to seize and flourish aloft. If you have a stockpile, given the poor quality of the so called "guerrillas" the militias et. al. attract, some pale-skinned scumbag will eventually rat you out to save his own wretched hide. You will lose your stockpile and your freedom. There will be no other result from stockpiling, because the fact that you stockpile indicates that you are not serious.

Yes, yes, I know the I.R.A. stockpiles guns and explosives. They also lose whole arsenals every year to the Gardai and the R.U.C., 150 Kalashnikovs at a time still in their original Libyan wrappings, that kind of thing. The I.R.A. stockpiles because they have a long ingrained love affair with guns almost as intense as that of the American right, although theirs is based on the long-standing British policy of prohibiting all Irish people from carrying weapons of any kind. They tend to overdo it for psychological reasons. But the Provos never have more than about *fifty people* on active service at any given time in the North and maybe a dozen or so on mainland Britain and in Europe; their ratios of talkers to doers is almost as bad as ours, although at least they do have a few fighters. They always have far more guns than they have men willing to pull the trigger.

Weapons of war in a truly insurrectionary movement do not belong in stockpiles, they belong in the hands of revolutionaries so the revolutionaries can use them and will not be caught unarmed. A serious guerrilla team parcels out the weapons and makes each man responsible for his own armament. Leave explosives alone unless you really, *really* know what the hell you're doing with them. The first explosives to start your people off with are hand grenades, not big huge truck bombs or strange concoctions your science nerd whips up in his basement. (Oklahoma City doesn't count; it is an exception to all rules until we know exactly who was responsible and why, which we probably never will.) Grenades are almost idiot-proof (which recommends them highly to American racial nationalists); properly used, grenades can be a devastating weapon of urban guerrilla warfare. Don't fool around with anything homemade.

4. You do not need fully automatic weapons.

Do not buy them. Do not stockpile them. Expel from your group immediately anyone who offers to procure them for you: he is a police agent. Unless you are properly trained in their use, machine guns are more dangerous to you than they are to the enemy. Machine guns are not toys with which you may play John Wayne on the Sands of Iwo Jima; I once saw a stupid nigger at Fort Jackson come very short because he'd watched too many movies and thought his M-60 was a toy. Given the mentality of many of our "freedom fighters", the urge for them to play with automatic weapons if you have them will be too great to resist.

Automatic weapons have two specific uses in military tactics. One is for the defense of established positions. The other is as part of a highly trained and properly led fire team, for use in fire-and-maneuver assaults. You are not going to be engaging in Rambo-like shoot-outs with police and troops, at least not more than once you won't. A large part of your guerrilla tactics will consist of striking at the enemy while avoiding such entrapments. You do not have that kind of skill and training level. (No, you don't.) You can accomplish anything you need to accomplish to attain the initial objectives of an insurrectionary movement with other weapons.

What weapons would those be? Friends, the most devastating personal weapon for hand to hand combat ever invented is the lowly *shotgun,* sawed off as short as possible. When you start accumulating your initial weapons stocks, buy shotguns and handguns, a few good rifles with high-powered scopes and a few good semi-autos. (SKSes are junk; avoid them, but most any other semi-auto long gun will serve). Buy these weapons legally and store them safely, but do not stockpile in barns or anything that hints at illegal intentions. Do not flourish them, display them, or let anyone know you have them. Do not buy guns in excessive quantity, and do not saw off your shotguns below the legal limit until the legal line has been breached and you're going to jail anyway.

5. The media and the police should not even know that you exist.

No press conferences, no press releases, no camera crews, no interviews, nothing that would tip your hand. When the time for direct action comes, the media are to be considered legitimate military targets. They are not our friends, not under any circumstances. Do not try to "use" them; they will use you.

Incredibly, the vast majority of American White "revolutionary" groups do not practice the most basic, rudimentary security precaution of all, keeping their membership *concealed from the enemy.* The worst possible catastrophe a fledgling guerrilla group can have is for one or more of its members to be identified by the government forces.

6. Do not wear uniforms of any kind.

If you do not understand why this is an absolute necessity, then do not attempt any kind of insurrectionary activity. You don't have sufficient intelligence to so do successfully.

7. Never defend! Attack!

The basic "strategy" of most militia groups, insofar as they have any (which isn't very far) is based on static defense of their communities. Against city niggers or outlaws in a time of total social breakdown, that may be a feasible goal. Against the Federal government of the United States—the most likely attacker of any White community—this outlook is absurd and suicidal. Again, this assumes with a *big* suspension of disbelief that the present "militias" would resist at all instead of throwing down their guns and blubbering to the D.A. for a plea bargain. Never, never, *never* allow yourself to be pinned down in a compound of any kind. You are facing the most overwhelming concentration of military and police power in human history. To be surrounded is the end. Period.

8. Do not rob banks.

Or commit other criminal fund-raising acts (like writing Freeman-style bad checks) until you have already established your revolutionary *bona fides* by several very high-profile attacks against the racial enemy. This appears to be what happened to the so-called "Aryan Revolutionary Army"; they wanted to be the Order but so far as is known never struck a blow at the enemy other than to rob banks containing the hard-earned money of White people which was insured by the FDIC. This is the worst possible publicity they could have received; thanks to these turkeys the public in the Northwest now views Christian Identity people as criminals and bank robbers. Thanks a lot, guys.

How do you raise your initial funds? I'll tell you how, and I'm not joking. *Sell the damned compound.* Use the money to buy transport, vans, RVs, trucks, vehicles which can transport men and weapons and supplies for small fire teams who will *move* and *strike* and then escape and evade, then strike again, etc. You do not need land or anything else which may lead to your getting surrounded. Land is useless to you. Either you will (most likely) die and not need it, or you will win and you can then appropriate all the land you want.

9. Establish an achievable political goal before you begin.

You are supposed to be guerrillas, not Natural Born Killers on some kind of pointless bloodbath crime spree. Violence is a *means* to an *end,* not an end in itself. One of the reasons the I.R.A. has failed is they've been taken over by common or garden variety gangsters and hate-mad psychos who have either forgotten this or never knew it.

10. The best idea yet: forget the whole thing.

We have completely wasted the past thirty years, comrades. That is a fact. Some of this wastage was due to sincere and hopeful expeditions down some dead ends which, in retrospect, were pretty obvious. The Duck Club and electoral politics are two examples which spring to mind. We have also been plagued with a series of self-appointed leaders who have been corrupt, incompetent, and dishonest, and we are still plagued with some of these holdovers from the past. You can yell and scream and moan and spread rumors that I'm a government agent all you want, but that's a fact as well. The Lord made most men out of clay, but he made most White racist leaders out of crap.

Had we not wasted those thirty years, it is possible that we might be in a position to engage in an armed insurrection against ZOG. We are not, and anyone who tells you otherwise is either a fool or a real police agent. I am telling you to get your heads together and learn. I am not asking you to die for your race. I am asking you to *live* for it, and more difficult, I am asking you to *work* for it.

I know this is a message many don't want to hear. For the sake of our future, folks, you'd best take heed.

[August 1998]

14th Century Economics Lesson

A long time Party supporter recently asked me to clarify a couple of points in the NSWPP Party Program, specifically the prohibition against usury. "Are you going to confiscate all individuals' life savings because they have earned interest?" The short answer, of course, is no, but it did remind me that we need to pay at least some attention to "the dismal science" of economics from an NS point of view. The nature of usury is a good place to start.

Before we can understand the National Socialist solution for the economic woes of capitalist society we must first understand the way our present form of usury-generated finance capitalism arose in the Middle Ages and early Renaissance period. Not for nothing is economics called "the dismal science"; it is not only a complex subject but usually pretty boring. Please bear with me; I'll try to keep this as simple and interesting as I can. I'm reading a book on Renaissance Italy at the moment, and it's inspired me to use a concrete example from the past to show how our present economic order developed. All this is going to be very greatly oversimplified, of course, but I hope it will help you understand one of the many long paths our people have taken to arrive at our present mess.

First off, you need to understand that although Karl Marx was full of sheep dip, he did recognize and articulate certain correct and vitally important things about the nature of capitalism. Capitalism is utterly dependent on the exploitation of human beings for their labor, and in order to function must reinvent Man as a commodity, an economic unit of production and consumption. This dehumanizing concept has proven one of the most destructive aspects of the Jewish incursion into Western civilization.

Secondly, capitalism is dependent for the generation of capital not

51

only on profit, but on the highly cost effective form of profit known as usury, the collection of interest on loaned money. Long recognized as the ultimate tool of Jewish power, usury was forbidden for centuries to Christians (which used to be pretty much the same thing as saying Aryans) by the Church. Only Jews were allowed to practice it and any Aryan found charging interest was subject to a variety of penalties ranging from fines to the public removal of bits and pieces of the offender's anatomy. Modern day banks would have you believe that the economy is entirely dependent on the charging of interest, but that's BS. The generation of non-production related profit through interest is actually a fairly recent development in man's economic history. So how did the economy work in the days before usury? A good case study would be the rise and fall of the great Lombard banking houses of Italy during the Middle Ages.

Okay: let's say we're in Venice, a great trading city, about the year 1396. Usury is forbidden to everyone except the Jews, and their interest rates are as high as 50%, so no one but a drunk or a madman deals with them; they exist on interest mostly off the very poor, as pawnbrokers, and the Church has even established a series of interest free co-op religious pawn shops to try and protect the poor from the bloodsuckers. But if you're a merchant you still have to finance your ventures, so how do you do it?

Let's say you want to send a ship to Constantinople full of Italian goodies, cloth and worked metal goods and glassware, wool, so forth and so on. You want to bring back the same ship full of Oriental goodies like spices, mahogany, Turkish rugs, etc. We will assign an arbitrary cost to this venture of 10,000 gold florins. You believe that the profit from the sale of your goods in Constantinople and the resale of their goods in Venice will yield 20,000 florins, which for the sake of argument we'll accept as accurate. Where do you get the money? You can put up the entire ten grand yourself if you're filthy rich, and many of the wealthiest merchant adventurers do, as well as putting up their lives, for many of these guys are not just businessmen, they're sea captains and explorers and occasional pirates, and they command their own vessels. They can opt to take all the risk, including the risk of the ship sinking or getting captured by pirates, and take all the profit. Or they can look for investors to share the risk.

Since our hypothetical merchant is a good Christian who doesn't want to deal with hebes and a good businessman who doesn't want to pay half his profit to (literally) a Shylock, he goes to one or more of the great Lombard banking houses, the Bardi, the Pazzi, the Strozzi, the Albizzi, or the up-and-coming Medici. These banks are centered mostly in Florence or Siena, but they have branches all over Europe in the days when the first Rothschilds are still haggling with peasants over the pawn of their wooden shoes for a few pfennig. Our merchant adventurer goes to the banks, most likely several of them because they will be more likely to back him if their individual exposure is less. He explains his venture, shows them the ship so they know it's a stout seaworthy vessel, lets them know he'll be captaining the voyage himself, and points out that he's got a good track record of a dozen prosperous expeditions prior to this. He looks good to the Lombards, and so they lend him the dough. The total outlay for this project is ten grand in gold florins. The merchant himself will put up 4,000 florins, or 40%. The Bardi, the Strozzi, and the Medici banks will put up 2,000 each. They know they will have to wait one year for the ship's return to find out how they did. This is the origin of the old expression "when my ship comes in."

If everything goes according to plan, the venture will bring 20,000 gold florins, thus recouping everyone's initial investment and leaving ten grand profit. The merchant will take four grand of the surplus and the three banks two grand each, a 100% return on their investment. Good business, and something comes of it when those who can afford it get a nice Persian rug or some pepper to put on Aunt Maria's lasagna, which in the days before refrigeration disguises the taste of the half-putrefied sausage she uses in her recipe. Of course it was all a lot more complicated than that. For instance, in many cases the ship's captain, if he was not the owner, would have a substantial share and the crew would be paid not only a minimum wage but a small share each as well, plus there was taxes and overhead just like today. But you get the idea. A rich merchant might send out ten ships a year under this system; three are lost but seven of them return, leaving an overall profit and Venetian society wealthier thereby.

Do you note the difference between this system and Jewish usury? The Lombard banking system was based on *productivity* for profit, whereas the Jewish usury system is a shell game where money multiplies by itself without relation to anything in the real world. Money was to be earned by buying actual things of value low and selling high, by making something or building something or undertaking risks to obtain something material and tangible. In this example, the objective was the importation of X amount of real consumer goods, not the manipulation of numbers on a piece of paper as in, say, today's stock exchange or commodities market where there is only the most tenuous connection, if any, between the arbitrary value of the paper and any real or valuable object or commodity. If the voyage didn't succeed, the investors were out their money, and this risk element led to a high degree of caution, canniness, and ability to assess risk as well as encouraged daring and enterprise for higher profits. The merchant princes of Renaissance Italy may have had a taste for luxurious living, intrigue, and poisoning one another, but they never threw money away like present day governments and multinationals. They had worked and sweated and bled and killed to get it. Another variation on this system was public works, for example the bridges over the river Arno in Florence, many of which were built by the bankers who were then allowed to collect tolls until they had recovered the expense of construction and a set profit—after which the bridges became free. There are endless variations: money was lent for agriculture, to build a factory or a workshop, to build a road, whatever, but always something you could touch, feel, taste, use or consume. Money did not magically produce money out of nothing as it does with usury.

So when did usury get its first foothold in the Western economy? Basically, when the Aryan ruling élite of that time, like their counterparts of the twentieth century, lost sight of their principles in the scramble for wealth and started acting like Jews. Unfortunately, the first big capitalist usurers in modern history were these same Lombard bankers in their later stages; the Jews then slid in on the coattails of the true claim that "everybody is doing it," and within a short time were running the whole game.

From the point of view of the lender, usury has one advantage over the productivity or venture-based system: it eliminates risk, for the lender, anyway. But it increases risk manyfold for the borrower who not only puts his business and his own capital on the line but sometimes everything he possesses. The borrower signs a bond or contract borrowing ten thousand florins and promising to pay back fifteen come what may, and as collateral he gives the lender the right to seize certain property if he is unable to pay by the stated date. The Lombard banking system was essentially a tool for the production of new wealth, while usury is a system for transferring existing wealth into a smaller number of hands, usually Jewish.

Essentially two things happened. First, a lot of the Lombard banks crashed down through the years when they inevitably made too many bad decisions, creating fewer and bigger banks handling more money led by more unscrupulous men as the Renaissance advanced. (Late Renaissance bankers and financial tycoons were often converted Jews, many of whom continued to practice Judaism in secret and openly favored their own people at the expense of their host nations.) Additionally, the Church became corrupt and quit enforcing the anti-usury statutes, and the secular princes and dukes and whatnot got into debt to the banks and overlooked the fact that they had begun to charge interest just like the Jews. U s u r y crept into our economy in stages, and it was still frowned upon even as late as the nineteenth century. (A character in a Sherlock Holmes story, for example, a ruined gambling nobleman who has mortgaged everything he owns and is about to lose it all, is referred to as being "in the hands of the Jews" by author Arthur Conan Doyle, an expression one could still get away with using as late as the 1890s.)Now, of course, we've got credit cards operating out of states like South Dakota with no banking laws to speak of who charge 24% revolving interest—it's actually cheaper to borrow money from the Mob, organized crime's traditional "vigorish" or interest rate being six for five or about 18%.

Another question I have been asked is about an NS Bulletin wherein I advocated a return to the gold standard. As most topics dealing with money seem to do, this also gets into the Jewish situation. *Plus d'argent, voici les Juifs,* as the French say.

Money was first invented as a substitute for barter, and for millennia consisted only of gold, silver, and occasionally copper or bronze coinage.

Eventually as trade expanded it became too cumbersome and dangerous to go on a trading expedition lugging long mule trains loaded with gold coin, so with the establishment of the first medieval banks the paper bank draft was invented, allowing a merchant in London to travel to Paris carrying only a document instead of heavy bags of money so tempting to bandits, do his business, deposit his profits in the Paris branch of the Bardi or whoever, and then draw them out again from the London branch when he got home. This was the first paper money, and it was specific, like a check made out to only one person.

Eventually the Lombard and later Jewish banks began to issue what today we would call negotiable securities or debentures—bank drafts for X amount of money with no name on them, which could be used as legal tender to buy, sell, pay, and lend. The practice of individual banks issuing their own paper money continued up until the beginning of this century; you can see all kinds of examples in museums. In the flourishing and expanding economy of a dynamic young America, private banks, states, cities, even railroads issued their own paper money. But these paper notes or bills were always gold or sometimes silver certificates—that is, if you had a ten dollar bill from the First National Bank of Philadelphia and you took it in to that bank, you had the right to get a ten dollar gold piece for it. Paper money was originally intended as a convenience, not as a substitute for precious metals.

Redeemability in gold or silver had one big advantage: it kept the money supply under control and pretty much eliminated the curse of inflation and insane interest rates. Almost all the inflationary spirals in the past, aside from the odd catastrophe like the Black Death, have had to do with the uncontrolled issue of paper money, i.e. the Continental Congress period, (my grandfather still used the expression "not worth a Continental,") Confederate money; the Weimar period in Germany, etc.

In 1913, this country did something so stupid that it defies rational analysis even today. We handed control of our money to the Jews in the form of a private corporation, the Federal Reserve, every head and important official of which from 1913 to this day has been Jewish. There is no such thing as U. S. currency, only Federal Reserve currency which is by law the only authorized form of legal tender. It took the Jews twenty years to take us off the gold standard and free themselves of the obligation to back up their green paper with gold or silver, but they managed it, and from 1934 onward the Jews have literally had a license to print money hand over fist. The more paper money there is in circulation, the higher interest rates are charged (and the more impossible it becomes for young White married people to buy a home.) It's all very complicated and I don't understand all the ins and outs of it myself, but basically the cause of the inflation and the insanely high cost of everything today is due to the Federal Reserve system using our money as a means to enrich world Jewry and loot the *Goldeneh Medina*—in Yiddish "The Golden Honeycomb," their word for America.

In the NS Bulletin I advocated a return to the gold standard as a temporary measure to get the money supply under control, reverse the wage-price spiral and get the cost of living under control, and to see if we can't slash the incredibly inflated cost of real property to the point where young couples can actually buy a home large enough to raise children in, not some crackerbox condo or renting until they're forty. What I would eventually like to see...

Ah, well, that's for another time.

Vive La Différence

If I had to pick the absolute worst thing that the Jews have done to us, I would say that they have driven a now almost insurmountable wedge between White men and White women. Nowhere else is the clearly genocidal and anti-human nature of Judaism more apparent. Nothing else has caused more suffering, anguish, disruption to Western civilization or loss to the world Aryan gene pool than the creation of a society where White men and women view one another as adversaries instead of partners. The instigation and propagation of this hatred between White men and women is their greatest success story, possibly in the long run a greater victory for Zionism than the destruction of the Third Reich or the creation of the artificial, criminal state of Israel, because when White men and women hate one another the number of White babies born drops like a stone and we get closer and closer to that point of no return where our racial extinction becomes inevitable. And always bear in mind that is the ultimate goal of the Jewish people—to exterminate every man and every *woman* with a White skin from the face of the earth.

But I'm not going to talk about that right now. I'm going to talk about my sex life.

Or rather, I am forced by the whole nature of this issue to open any discussion of it with a lengthy "full disclosure" statement. There is an overriding reason for this, and that is the nature of the ridiculous zoo which we so laughably call the Movement. My views on women in society are entirely racial and political, they are methodically and carefully thought out, but not one in ten of you are going to accept that. In the immature, inane, politically powerless, politically retarded and neurotic tendency we refer to as "the Movement", any recognition of *political principle* in the commonly accepted sense of the term is almost non-existent. Because we are by and large weak, neurotic, and mentally paralyzed units of production and consumption instead of men and women, with us *everything is personal.* Always, *always* personal. The concepts of loyal opposition and constructive criticism simply don't exist in the Bowel Movement. Any criticism, no matter how well founded or how well intended, is taken as a deadly insult and the immediate response is to attack the critic and impugn his motives for saying whatever he is saying, rather than consider its content or validity.

We are, in short, a *feminine* movement, an odd thing for me to say in view of the topic for tonight, but true, when you think about it. It is ironic that we should be accused by our female comrades of being Neanderthal woman-haters who want to bash them on the head, drag them to the bedroom and after we finish there chain them to the stove so they can't get into the voting booth. Frankly, we could do with some more guys of that type than we have. With the exception of certain localized sects of the Ku Klux Klan who operate in areas of the rural South largely untouched by Political Correctness as yet, a visit to your typical rightwing or racist meeting in a rented motel banquet room hardly reveals a ravening band of tattooed Road Warriors ready to rumble with the bike chains and slavering lasciviously over the waitresses.

Generally, right wing and racist groups have a membership which is 95% male; about 60% over the age of 50 and 85% over the age of 30; and who consist of very elderly conservatives, middle-aged men with big bellies and two or three divorces under their expansive belts; and a third type predominant in the National Alliance and other "intellectual" racial groups: youngish to middle-aged men, thin to the point of being gaunt often due to strange dietary habits or health problems; with strange rolling eyeballs and facial tics; either obsessively neat and dressed like undertakers or else smelling like goats due to non-bathing; and generally with some very, very strange ideas on a lot of subjects, including women. *[Do you see now why people like Pierce and Metzger get apoplectic over Horrible Harold? We're not supposed to say things like this is public, however true it might be, never mind try to change all this like Horrible Harold does. And yes, this is germane to the women issue. Bear with me, please.]*

Anyway, when I speak of my purely political and racial National Socialist views on the subject—and yes, that is what they are—as in

59

everything else I try to advocate, I am going to be accused by the Usual Suspects of saying these things because I myself am sexually weird or repressed or I allegedly can't get girl friends or some such effluvia. Our female comrades, who are presently most of them in a state of high dudgeon with Your Friend and Humble Gensec, are going to say the same thing, something to the effect of "No wonder you're not married; you don't know how to treat a woman, you're a failure as a man, etc." In every case this will be an effort to avoid dealing with *what* I am saying, which is par for the course in the "Movement".

But this topic is *important,* as I have stated before. Unlike religion it is *solvable,* if we can somehow re-acquire the art of thinking instead of feeling and thinking right at that, and unlike religion it must be thrashed out and solved *now,* not put aside for the time after the revolution when we have power. So in order to clear away and hopefully stop-punch the vicious personal attacks which will result from my assertion of what I believe to be clear and evident political and racial truths, I am going to give as brief as possible a history of my own relations with the Fair Sex.

* * *

I will be 45 years old in September. In my time I have had three very serious relationships, including two marriages, four or five semi-serious relationships, and possibly a total of about two dozen casual relationships and or one-night stands, including one prostitute whom I picked up purely for the sake of saying I had done it. My attitude towards prostitutes is similar to that of Voltaire, who was invited by the Marquis de Sade to participate in an orgy, which he did with such great vim and vigor that the Divine Marquis asked him to attend another such event. The philosopher declined, saying, "Once was legitimate intellectual curiosity. Twice would be perversion."

I think my sexual past is probably about average for a man of my age in the times in which I live. I have never bought into the "Playboy philosophy" that a man is somehow less than a man if he doesn't go leaping from bed to different bed every couple of nights. This has spared me a hell of a lot of grief. Usually relationships with women have been fairly low on my list of "things to do" at any given time in my life. There are some who think this makes me odd. Screw them. They are idiots. Human beings have other purposes in this world other than to engage in endless acts of copulation with as many partners as possible. Animals can do that. We are more than animals.

In junior high school and high school I had the usual going steady type relationships, although fewer than the average. Many of the kids were constantly involved with a string of adolescents from the time they were twelve; I was never in that league, nor did I make plays for the cheerleaders or the overdeveloped sexpots with the hot reputations. (This was back in the Brady Bunch days, remember. I actually remember sock hops, the Beatles, and bell bottoms.) Not only was I unable to compete with the jocks and the BMOCs, but that super-model type simply didn't attract me, and still doesn't. I tended to hang on the outskirts of the female herd and pick off the stragglers, so to speak, the girls who walked through the halls alone and not with a standard gaggle of five or six other girls, the skinny ones with glasses and long, straight hair, a bit of acne and straight-A averages, you get the idea. The result was that I got my share of stolen kisses in the band room and fumbling feels under the bleachers, but I was plagued with a lot of just plain, pesky *bad luck*. Not to mention the girls themselves having worse luck, lest you think I'm a totally insensitive clod.

The first girl I ever "went all the way" with, as we said in those days, I got pregnant. We were both thirteen years old when it happened and 14 when the baby was born and given up for adoption. I still have a daughter somewhere who turned 30 in May; it's odd that I may be the father of an Ally McBeal someplace. The second one, a hillbilly Lolita from Tennessee, gave me a dose of syphilis, and I had to cop a fake UNC student idea and go to the medical clinic on campus for almost a year for injections and check-ups. That mountain dew must have been powerful stuff; for years afterwards at every checkup I was told something called "titers" still showed up in my blood. The girl I was unofficially engaged to in my senior year was killed in an automobile wreck one week after we graduated from high school in 1971; I was in Florida, her hippy-dippy and/or preppie friends hated my guts and didn't bother to inform me, so I missed her funeral. I was batting a thousand, I can tell you. By the by, for those of you who are utterly fascinated by the story of Harold's weird and wonderful yoot, I recommend you order my novel *Fire and Rain,* set in Chapel Hill. Parts of it are autobiographical.

I have been married two and a half times to an eclectic set of ladies, one American, one Irish, and one New Zealander. I therefore have enough practical experience to understand that every man/woman relationship is different and it is dangerous to try and generalize, although not impossible. There are certain common themes, especially in today's society where everyone hangs their most intimate details in their private lives out to dry for the National Inquirer and Oprah, but every individual case is unique.

My first marriage was a teenaged mistake. I was 19, Lucie was 18. We neither of us had any business getting married, and we *damned* sure had no business getting married to each other. That one lasted about five years, from 1972 to 1977, and we were separated for the last eighteen months or so of that. I put Lucie through a lot, dragging her to Rhodesia with me, and we lost one baby by miscarriage and another died at age 4 months from a viral infection when I was stationed at Llewellin Barracks, Bulawayo. Chalk up another victim for sanctions; we got our water from the Umgusa River and were constantly being told by the base command to boil it when the ancient purification plant broke down and no spare parts were available. Lucie had a mental breakdown after the baby died and for a time was locked up in the rubber room at Ingutsheni; I was off in the bush half the time and off doing stuff for the Rhodesia White People's Party or SAFOM the other half, not to mention being drunk most of the time (which is the normal Rhodesian condition) and I wasn't much help.

You see that I am perfectly willing to take responsibility for the bulk of this particular failed marriage, although if we'd stayed in the States I doubt we would have made it either. Lucie and I did spend one weekend together in the spring of 1980 after the divorce, when she flew down from Chicago. I dropped her off at the airport on Monday to fly back to Chicago, wished her cheerio, and we both said, "We must do this again sometime," but we knew we never would. We actually had a pretty good time, and I was glad we were able to "obtain closure" as today's psychobabble calls it. One final comment on the Lucie Era: the bedroom was the one place where we *did* get along, and I can tell you from personal experience that you can't keep a marriage going purely on the basis of sex.

My next marriage in Ireland came apart for two reasons. First off, my incredibly bizarre family situation in North Carolina became involved and entangled in my marriage through my Irish children and their legal rights to one of the largest privately held fortunes in the South, which is something I don't intend to get into here. Suffice it to say that if the story of my family were made into a TV series it would be about one third *Dallas,* one third *Millennium,* and one third *Married With Children.* Or maybe *Leave It To Beaver Meets The Borgias.* Or possibly *The Simpsons Halloween Special On Speed* if you tried to animate it. (Hell, I suppose I'd better shut up before some Jew writer in Hollywood decides he wants to do a few pilot episodes.) Order *Fire and Rain* if you're curious; the sub rosa tale is pretty much all there. Where was I? Oh, yes, Louise. Well, the second reason Louise and I broke up, long run, is the most ancient of all male-female conflicts: who wears the pants in the family. I did, but Louise never stopped trying to seize the wheel. What infuriated her (and other women I have lived with) is she couldn't make me angry. I never raise my voice during an argument. I use words rather than decibels, and if and when the situation gets out of hand and it is obvious that nothing is to be gained by continuing, I simply tell her I will not discuss the matter further under those conditions and I leave the house. This, of course, drives them crazy. It took me a long time to realize that if you really love her and want to keep her you don't want to drive her crazy.

I have never been one for scenes, shouting, threatening, name calling, etc. When I am confronted with a female partner who is having a hissy fit over something I try to talk it out with her at first. I won't say *reason* it out, because I know full well that nine times out of ten reason has nothing to do with the real problem and the subject under discussion is *not* why she is really unhappy—I have at least learned that much about women down through the years. Many men make the mistake of trying to convince their women one way or the other with reason and logic on the subject of discussion; usually that's not what the problem is about, and the men end up baffled and hurt because they don't understand why nothing they say or do seems to make any difference.

Good example: time after time Movement men come to me and bang

63

my ear about their troubles with their wives or girl friends who are giving them grief over their racial involvement, usually with the final ultimatum to choose between them. "Lips that touch racism will never touch mine," blah, blah, blah. In most cases, that's *not what it's about.* What it is about is that she senses a rival for your time, effort, money, and affection. It would be the same with anything you were devoted to that intensely: fishing, Establishment politics or a vocation like being a cop (cops have this problem a lot), an artistic vocation like painting or writing (I get a lot of typewriter jealousy from my ladies), anything like that. *She* demands to be the center of your entire existence—and in today's politically correct world, she has been taught that she has the *right* to make that demand and that *you* are at fault if you do not accede to it.

Sorry, I'm getting off the track here again; all of these things are for future installments of what promises to be a long series. Anyway, my marriage to Louise might have survived our personality conflicts, or it might have survived my father's assorted conspiracies to cheat my children out of their rightful inheritance, but it could not survive both and didn't. I'll take about 25% of the blame for the failure of this one—I should never have married her in the first place. Louise needs to take about 25%, and the Prince of Darkness from the cypress swamps needs to take the other half. What was bad about this one is that four innocent children got caught in the crossfire, so yes, when you hear me pontificating about women, bear in mind I have had that experience as well.

Jan from New Zealand I do not propose to discuss; her I loved, and she was taken from me by the evil which I continue to battle to this day in all those e-mails and newsletters which some of you tell me you do not want to hear. All I can say is that while I do not deny my many personal motives in battling the thread of vileness and corruption in the Movement which begins with Benny Klassen and continues down to the present day in the person of a few involved individuals, I do not believe those motivations disqualify me from fighting that vileness or invalidate what I have to say. Because one is personally victimized by evil, does that mean one can never speak out against it because one is not "objective?"

There have been other semi-serious relationships. Judy the Holy Roller was a true Southern lady, but those Jesus freaks did a number on her head you wouldn't believe, and I am sure some of you have had *that* happen to you. The Tattooed Lady of Rockwell Hall has become something of a legend, as has Barbara the Drunk who streaked one of Glenn Miller's rallies. Eileen from Donegal and Mary from Cork were two who got away and I'll always wonder what might have been. (By the by, as a totally irrelevant aside, I have noticed that when a man is married, all of a sudden other married women start coming on to him. Has anybody else had that experience? Sorry, digressing again.)

In the post-Jan era I've slowed down; I have had two more or less casual relationships with female co-workers at my several places of employment and one platonic friendship with a really fine thing in Seattle who was one of those *real* cases where some bastard first husband beat her black and blue and used her like a doormat, and she couldn't bear to be touched physically by a man. (I have found that most of these stories gain a lot in the telling, but not all, and don't have a fit, ladies, I am *not* claiming that men never abuse women. I know they do.)

For those of you who are just insatiably curious about the physical side of my career as a Lothario, go take a cold shower. I am not Bill Clinton, I am not a locker room jock, I show respect for my ladies and I do not talk about intimate subjects like that. It is my experience that sex is like combat in the military: the more a man boasts about it, the less of it he has actually done. I will give you one hint: it's the little things that count with women. A single rose is not only less expensive than a whole sheaf, it is more effective, at least with the kind of lady I become involved with. I do not try to seduce women or get them parked on a lonely lane and start pawing them, nor do I drop my drawers like Bill Clinton and say "Kiss that thang, honey!" My technique, if you want to call it that, is very simple. I *take my time.* Softlee, softlee, catchee monkey. I listen to them, I become their friends first, I get them to like me as a person, and then I *ask.* I find it works about 50% of the time. In all of my teenaged and adult life, I have only had one woman blow up on me when I popped the question, which when you consider the readiness of women to fly off the handle over these things, is not doing too shabby, I think. What other technique do you know of that can claim a 50% success rate?

And if it doesn't work, remember this: a gentleman can always take no for an answer. A man who forces his attentions on a woman after she has clearly indicated that she is not interested is a damned pig.

Some people have asked if I tried to put the moves on Christy at UNC, the one I wrote about in 1996. The answer is no. I honestly believe that it is undignified and unfair for a man of my age to pursue women young enough to be their daughters; obviously our Illustrious Head of State disagrees. Others have asked if the demented Sharon Mooney was ever my girlfriend. The answer is no; I only met her once and it was obvious to me she was so badly mentally and emotionally damaged that she was virtually useless to the Movement; besides, she was too young for me. The National Alliance have circulated some alleged letters I wrote to her, part of which seem to be legit and the key sections of which are forged, which is in keeping with the Pierce cult's standard practice.

The last affair I had was in Chapel Hill where I became involved with a *really* beautiful Russian woman, a grad student, whom I might add already had her green card and who therefore didn't need an American husband to get one. Anna seemed amenable to a permanent relationship, although it was always tentative; she made it clear she wanted me to get a normal j ob and bring in a much bigger buck, which was fair enough from her point of view. She had no qualms about National Socialism, being very Jew-aware herself as most Eastern Europeans are, and one of her major pluses was that we could discuss racial politics freely. She once told me, "Three of my family were killed by the Germans during the war. Over fifty were killed by Stalin."

This relationship ended after the malicious lawsuit began and it became clear that I was being stalked by a psychopath. It has been suggested to me that one of the reasons Willard hates me so is that he feared my possible success with a Russian lady while his own Russian mail order bride left him after being used as a punching bag once too often. I do not know how he could have found out about Anna, but I do know he had private detectives on me in the late summer and early autumn of 1996, so it is possible he did. I had no intention of giving up the Party, and after things like vandalized mailboxes and feces on my doorstep I sat Anna down and told her that I would not hurt her in the way I hurt many of my other ladies, by involving her in the insanity which seems inescapably to accompany my way of life. One of the reasons I am so passionate about our Movement changing our ways is so that we can create a kind of subculture or world of our own wherein it *is* possible for our people to have some kind of normal life. I have got lawsuits, contempt of court warrants, telephone threats, vandalism, whole websites on the Internet smearing me, NA weirdos creeping up to my windows at night trying to videotape me naked, phony websites being put up allegedly showing me committing homosexual acts, weird psychotics who have shrines of hate in their homes where they burn candles before my picture and babble to themselves, plus of course what ZOG itself may dish out to me some day when it finds out these tactics do not work. I am as poor as a church mouse, and not being dishonest like Pierce or Metzger there is no chance I will ever be able to offer a woman 345 rolling acres and a Bavarian hunting lodge built on my supporters' donations. In all good conscience, I cannot ask any woman to share this life and no longer have any intention of doing so.

* * *

I have been asked where the above famous expression "vive la différence" came from. I understand it happened thus:

In the 1890s France was considering giving women the vote, and some famous French feminist whose name I can't recall was given the honor, almost unique for a woman at that time, of addressing the National Assembly in full session, all male of course, and all of whom sat there attired in their full formal dress suits with the white gloves, wide shoulder sashes, decorations, top hats and other such 1890s politicians' fripperies. The lady was up on the podium haranguing them with her feminist rap, which was listened to in polite silence. She concluded her speech with "Really, monsieurs, you must acknowledge that when one comes right down to it, there is very little difference between men and women." At this remark, the entire chamber spontaneously rose to its feet as one man, and shouted out, *"Vive la différence!"*

Men and women are *different*. Not inherently inferior or superior to one another, but *different*. To say that one sex is in any way inferior or superior to another is like saying that apples are inferior to oranges or vice versa. They are two different fruits and any such comments are a matter of personal taste and outlook, not scientific or pragmatic fact. To say that an apple is in some way "better" or worse than an orange has no relevance or meaning in the real world. The differences between men and women are about 20% environmental and psychological, that 20% being subject to a certain limited degree of possible manipulation and alteration but by no means as much so as feminists would like to have us believe, and about 80% biological, physical, and biochemical. It is therefore pointless and absurd to try and create in men and women two "equal" humanoid organisms. It cannot be done.

Men, on the whole, are physically larger and stronger than women. Yes, there are individual exceptions, more so in today's politically correct culture as White males degenerate into Dilbert-esque cubicle dwellers and women become more masculine in character, which seems to somewhat augment their physical size. One of the most sinister developments in recent years have been several statistical surveys and studies indicating that sedentary American White males are actually losing their virility in the physical as well as the moral sense; White sperm counts have been dropping for almost twenty years. We are becoming less than men in every sense of the word.

But in all non-yuppie, more or less organic societies of all races, men are as a rule the larger and stronger. Some of this has to do with diet. In any business or work environment where there are large numbers of illegal aliens, for example, compare the size of Orientals who were born and raised in China or Southeast Asia on nothing but rice and a little fish with the size and weight of Asian-Americans who were born here and grew up on plenty of fruits, grains, vegetables, and good old-fashioned cholesterol-packed *meat.* Native-born Chinese women especially are tiny things, between seventy and eighty pounds, although actually stronger than native-born White valley girls due to having been forced into manual labor from birth. But most of these exceptions are individual, culture-specific, or otherwise idiosyncratic. Men are physically bigger and stronger than women. This is because Nature has given human men and women a natural division of labor, one which cannot be repealed by feminism, by affirmative action, or by anything else. That natural division is simple: the man provides the food, the shelter, and the protection from enemies for the family unit. The woman bears and raises the children. This is how human beings are supposed to live; indeed, the only way they *can* live past a couple of confused and chaotic generations of the kind we are experiencing now. It is innate. It is biological. It cannot be changed, and any attempt to tamper with it produces disaster and destruction, as we are now learning in Politically Correct America.

No baby creatures are more helpless than human infants. Snakes and alligators are self-sufficient from the time they hatch, birds and kittens and puppies are up and functioning and providing their own food in a matter of weeks. Human babies must be fed initially by a mother's milk for a period of months, and then on specially treated and prepared food for another year or so. They cannot defend themselves or escape from an enemy unaided. Children cannot really live on their own with any hope of survival for the first ten or eleven years of life. The whole "traditional nuclear family" so hated and railed at by liberals and feminists is an institution ordained by God/gods/Nature/The Force/the Great Pumpkin or whatever to make sure that the human species continues to exist. The primary purpose of the man-woman relationship is to produce children and care for them until they are adult enough to fend for themselves. The emotional and cultural side benefits to marriage are valuable and have produced our whole civilization, but they are in fact incidental by-products of the central process of continuing the human species. The father and the mother are not the most vital part of the picture, although they are essential: the children are.

This arrangement is not unknown in other species, and in all mammals at any rate the male is always larger, stronger, faster, and more combative. In many cases, such as lions and wolves, one alpha male practices polygamy with a number of females and kills off other male competitors until he grows old and weak and is in turn killed off by a younger male. Primitive non-White societies in Africa and the Third World still follow this pattern. Aryans, for the most part, have generally mated for life down through the years; there are some records of polygamy in ancient Aryan cultures but not as many as elsewhere. The ancient Norse and Germans practiced it, but gave it up about the turn of the last millennium. For good or for ill, once the Aryan race became Christianized, polygamy vanished. (No comments about Mormons, please; they are not typical and their polygamy is not organically rooted

69

in history but in conscious chosen behavior.) One reason for polygamy was extremely high male mortality rates in time of war; an interesting modern example from the Third World is Saddam Hussein awarding large cash bonuses, automobiles, and homes to Iraqi officers who take a widow from the Iranian or American wars as their second or third wife. The Iraqi gene pool has been decimated by the slaughter of almost twenty years of continuous warfare, and Saddam is quite open about his determination to ensure that Iraq is not depopulated. I wish to hell Germany had created some similar kind of polygamy status after both World Wars.

Men and women are two halves of a whole. Neither can or should exist without the other. The idea of two halves of the same organism competing with one another, dominating one another, or existing in enmity with one another is an obvious recipe for destruction. This is why the Jews promote the idea that men are some kind of natural enemy to women, as they promote any and all things which are destructive and poisonous and breed confusion and unhappiness among our people. They hate us and want us all dead, and they use every weapon they can to bring this about, including feminism. Quite simple, really.

Homosexuality is a loathsome perversion. It is absolutely and utterly wrong, because it denies the natural division of labor between man and woman and because it precludes the production of children. The instinctive loathing that the overwhelming majority of normal people feel even today for faggots and dykes is an inner recognition on the part of our genetic makeup (or souls, if you are Christian) that what is going on is unnatural and counter-survival (or sinful). This is why politically correct brainwashing and social engineering, relatively successful in obtaining a grudging acceptance of mud people as equals, seems largely to have floundered when trying mentally and emotionally to coerce people into accepting the open practice of sodomy. This is especially true when it involves a sodomitic threat to children: Whites are still capable of anger and action when the local school board tries to bring in *Heather Has Two Mommies,* about the only thing left they *will* react to. Millions of years of genetic codes triggering biological survival behavior cannot be overwritten by fifty years of Hollywood propaganda or suppressed by hate speech laws.

National Socialism seeks to re-create a world based on natural order, and that most specifically includes, as it did in Germany, a return to what are referred to as traditional family values, with the gainfully employed father as the head of the family and the full-time mother and homemaker as the family's heart. This does not in any way involve enslaving women; in the very real sense it *liberates* them from feminism and Judaic values and the true slavery of the marketplace. The Aryan women of the future will have a freedom which they have all but lost today—the freedom to be real women.

What largely Jewish and lesbian feminists want, claim, or advocate is not relevant to anything in the real world. They more than liberals as a whole are doomed to eventual defeat and disappointment, however much they may have achieved a very temporary and very slight, superficial success in the English speaking world. Feminism is essentially a form of sexual perversion, because it distorts what is natural in the sexual roles of men and women. Feminism, like integration and all forms of liberalism, can only be imposed on both men and women at the point of a gun, literally or economically.

Remove the force of ZOG's law and the economic necessity for women to work simply to make ends meet, and feminism like racial integration will die.

But What Should We DO, Harold?

On Saturday, February 6th, I received a four-page letter in the mail from a reader in South Carolina, which I feel requires a response. I will not reproduce her letter here because I do not have her permission to do so, because it is too long, and also because a point by point commentary similar to that I provided to another correspondent a while back might end up generating more heat than light.

The thrust of her letter is twofold: first off, she complains that I do not "explain exactly what it is that I want White people to do," and second she tells me that I have failed, that there is no point in continuing to fight on, and I must discontinue sending her letters and e-mails which disturb and upset her by asking her to give her attention to topics which cause her pain and distress and which she does not wish to think about. (She says it pretty much in those words, and her frankness does her credit.) She adds that in accordance with a long-standing rite-wing practice, she is joining the lemming-like rush to the latest Great White Hope, a phenomenon that experienced activists will be familiar with. Every few years a Man On A White Horse appears (Pat Buchanan being a good example) who promises White folks he will do what we ourselves dare not attempt, and he will demand nothing of us except money and applause. We then rush to him like charging lemmings. The latest Great White Hope in this case is David Duke, who is riding the crest of a wave with the publication of his autobiography *My Awakening.*

And before you ask, if you're into Great White Hopes, I think you could do a lot worse than Duke. Hell, we *have* done a lot worse. Duke at least still believes in the Aryan racial cause and he has managed to tap dance through the Movement minefield without getting sucked into the kind of Fed/Jew trap involving compromise, corruption, and betrayal which destroyed Metzger and Pierce as human beings, although Duke came damned close over that Dominica business in 1981. After Ed Fields, David Duke is pretty much the best of the 1970s crowd still standing, so by all means, folks, rush to him with as many "oooohs!" and "aaaahs!" as you care to vociferate. I am actually quite interested in observing the techniques the power structure will use to screw Duke out of a Congressional seat, which everyone including the news media admits he could win hands down in an honest election. The idea that there is any remaining utility for the White man in the electoral system is of itself absurd, but elections can still serve a certain propaganda function. If I can ever get anyone interested, I might try it myself again sometime in the future. The problem is that it would be impossible for me to run an election campaign without someone going to the inconvenience of actually coming here to Texarkana and helping. Raising the Titanic seems to be a likelier proposition.

Where was I? Oh, yes, I was responding to the South Carolina lady's letter. Because of the length involved I will have to paraphrase what she says, point by point. I will try to do so fairly and accurately. I am not trying in any way to denigrate or insult this lady; her view is actually representative to some degree of a common attitude in the Movement.

There Once Was A Book...

I get this question of "What do you actually want us to do?" a lot, from people who keep urging me to be "positive" and "upbeat". I want you to do three things, which I will go over with you in a minute.

It is one of the minor mysteries of the Movement why my answer never seems to register. On thinking back over the past five years, I find I have answered this question at least two dozen times, four or five times in print and at least twenty times in e-mails, C-Grams, etc. I answer this question in varying degrees of detail, and within a week or so I am once more getting plaintive calls of "But what do you want us to *do,* Harold?" Sometimes I hear this within 48 hours of having answered it. The reason, I think, is that what I ask of you (collective Movement "you") demands that you incur some degree of risk and personal inconvenience. The White male has an astounding ability simply to tune out facts, ideas, or

73

situations he doesn't wish to deal with. If he doesn't like the program, he reacts in typical Middle American fashion: he picks up the remote and he changes the channel. You ask, I explain, you don't like what you hear, so you change the channel until the next time you ask the question.

The first thing I should point out is that for the entire five years of the existence of the NSWPP Mark II, we had something called a Party Manual which explained, very carefully, in detail and with precision, just exactly what it was I meant by the phrase "getting up off your butts" and what I wanted you to do in order to assume your fair share of the racial burden of struggle and resistance. The manual explained how to go about setting up a Party unit, what equipment you would need, what activities you should engage in, how to deal with media, how to conduct yourself if and when you were arrested, etc. More importantly, the manual explained what you should *not* do, to try and help you avoid the mistakes of the past. The second edition of that manual established a Party organizational structure based on the combined experiences of two of the most successful underground organizations in the world, La Cosa Nostra and the Irish Republican Army.

Hundreds of copies of this manual were distributed, mostly for free, over the five year period of the NSWPP's activity. With one noble and notable exception, the Party Manual was completely ignored. The one exception was Comrade Wagner of Fort Worth, Texas, who for over two years established and ran an almost textbook classic, superbly organized and motivated Party cell of four men, following the manual almost to the letter. The results he achieved were spectacular; as I recall, something on the order of 100,000 leaflets and stickers were distributed, our Fort Worth White Power Hotline made national news more than once and kept shorting out phone company equipment when some popular messages got over 10,000 calls per hour. The only major media publicity the second NSWPP got was in Fort Worth. Once again our Movement received a living demonstration that one single dedicated man can move mountains. This was a man who, I might add, had every legitimate personal and medical and financial reason to stay out of the fight personally, far more reason than just about any one else ever had. The unit only ceased activity when Wagner's health made it utterly impossible for him to continue; you can't run a political insurgency from the intensive care unit of a hospital.

74

What ever happened to the rest of those hundreds of Party Manuals? They sit in hundreds of drawers, gathering dust, or possibly in some cases hold pride of place in secret collections of racial material deep in the recesses of some middle-class basement or den or rec room, to be taken out and displayed only to one or two close acquaintances, almost in the manner of old men in dirty raincoats sharing pieces of pornography. "See!" I can hear the excited whisper. "There it is! I told you! A real swastika! Oh be still, my throbbing heart!"

Eventually I reduced the whole "what to do?" question to three simple, basic assignments. Practically speaking, I think these three things are all we can reasonably expect of the human material we presently have access to, but by God, I think that our once noble Race at least has the right to expect these three things of someone who knows the truth! For the record, here again are the three things I want you to do in order to fulfill your racial duty.

I. Speak. I want you to speak to your fellow White people about race, about the Jews, about Adolf Hitler, about the glory and pride of their own race. I want you to confront evil and political correctness openly by speaking out against it, in your workplace, in your schools, in your churches, wherever evil and hatred for White culture and civilization lurks. I do not ask that you take this to ridiculous lengths. I do not ask that you get up on a table in your break room and harangue your fellow workers or make a nuisance of yourself. I do not want you to come across as a crank. But every one of your co-workers and every member of your family and everyone that you associate with should know your political and racial views, and you should be ready, willing, and able to defend your race and your heritage and the Third Reich and whatever else needs defending at the drop of a hat.

Remember: *silence is complicity.* When you allow evil to pass unremarked, uncriticized, and unrefuted, then you are accessory to that evil, and to allow oneself to become an accessory to evil through silence is the act of a coward. Show some damned courage! When confronted with Political Correctness, *step forward,* openly in public, where others can see you and know your name, and say out loud "This is wrong! I cannot stop it, but I will not let it pass in silence." Ours is a silent genocide and it depends on silence to succeed. We are where we are today largely because the White male has rolled over and played dead. Be a man! Break the silence!

II. Meet. The most appalling Movement development in recent years, to my mind, is the idea we've acquired that we can do it all while hiding behind a nice, safe, anonymous computer. The introduction of the Internet has proven to be the death knell of the last remaining rudimentary physical activity that White racialists would undertake in a standing position out of doors, simple literature distribution. Almost no one does it any more; White males (as opposed to men) sit at home with a cold brewski in their hands and play with their computers.

The subject of the internet is one which I am going to have to address at some length later on, but for now suffice it to say that it gives us the safe option of interacting with a *machine* instead of with other fallible human beings who might end up entangling and complicating our lives in various ways. Like so many Dilberts, White males have become so afraid of any human contact that we flee into the cubicle and the computer screen, another act of cowardice, because only a coward flees from the rough and tumble of human emotion, human fellowship, and human conflict. I have always felt that one of the most damning indictments against Bill Pierce is his flight into the mountains of West Virginia to *get away from his own people,* a deliberate attempt to make himself as inaccessible and hard to find as possible so he is seldom compelled to deal with his own supporters on a face to face basis, or answer awkward questions he does not wish to discuss about certain of his questionable associations, the source of some of his income, etc. I have more than one first-hand account of people driving a thousand miles to meet The Great Man Himself and then when they get to the gates of the West Virginia compound, he refused to see them. Contrast my own constant urging for as many of you as possible to come and meet me personally, even to the point where I moved to a central geographic location on a major interstate to make it easier for you.

No, people, one cannot bring about political or social change from behind a computer any more than one can bring it about from behind a post office box. For there to be any organized racial resistance, racially aware Whites must *meet* with one another physically, look one another in the eye, become friends and comrades and offer one another mutual

76

support and reinforcement, must work and plan and bond together as friends, neighbors, brothers and sisters, and socialize with one another in the widest sense of the term.

One of the worst criticisms of our Movement, because it is so true, is that it is impossible for single White males to find a mate in our own circles. One of several reasons for this is our retreat from any personal or human contact of any kind. How can we bring White women around when we make no attempt to bring other White men around? The prototypical White Dilbert's ancestors ruled this planet as kings; today Dilbert hides in his cubicle, turning inward on himself and his still superior knowledge to create his own little virtual world in the computer, or in books, or in the pointless quasi-Nordic mysticism of neo-paganism. The White male needs to get his ass back out into the real world and learn the lost art of dealing with flesh and blood human beings again.

Time and again in the NSWPP I got e-mails and letters, often from some young White boy or girl convinced they were all alone in their racial agony, literally *begging* me to give them the names and addresses of someone in their area that they could physically meet in order to provide some kind of White contact and support in their despair and isolation in the Politically Correct world. Time and again there would be so-called "comrades" living within half an hour's drive of this person who reacted with anger and paranoia to even the suggestion that they step forward and meet with another White in order to further the cause which they claimed to support. More than once I got hysterical e-mails demanding to be removed from the mailing list and all trace of their association with the Party destroyed, because my request that they take the rudimentary action of meeting someone else in a restaurant in order to serve their race convinced them that I was some kind of agent provocateur. The number of White people, especially young people, whom we have lost because other so-called "National Socialists" were such chickenshit cowards, is something that I don't even want to think about. Dozens, at least.

It has been suggested that in any new party I create formal memberships and be rigorous about enforcing the minimal financial commitment of dues. I am of the opinion that if and when any new party is ever formed it must be made clear that Aryan honor and integrity must demand from every member at least some minimum degree of personal, physical courage, and this should be expressed in the understanding that by joining the Party one is agreeing to have one's name and contact address given out and to *meet* with other people to act as a recruiter. We have to begin teaching discipline, integrity and self worth to our people; we must begin to weed out the contemptible cowardice that pervades the male members of our race like a spiritual leprosy. I ask no one to do pointless, stupid and counterproductive things, but meeting with other White people to provide them with moral support and comradeship is not a stupid and pointless thing; it is the first step towards building a true Resistance.

III. Resist. I probably haven't emphasized this third point enough. By "resist" I mean that I ask you to commit all manner of overt acts which harass, annoy, demoralize, confuse, or distract the racial enemy. The left and environmental whackos refer to this as "monkeywrenching", which is a term I think we need to steal. I ask you to display not only courage but imagination, resourcefulness, subtlety, intelligence, planning, patience, alertness and observation, all the virtues of the revolutionary, and **strike back!** Why, exactly, must White people acquiesce passively in our own destruction? We not only bow down to our murderers, we pay for the bullets which kill us, figuratively speaking. Our tax dollars, our creativity, our labor, and our loyalty have been placed at the service of the government and the alien parasites who are draining the blood from our veins. Why do we have to *help* the Zionists and liberals by maintaining the very system which is poisoning our minds, bodies, and souls unto death? It is something which, to me, is so obvious that I am rather surprised I should even have to mention it, but apparently I do.

Every oppressed people down through history, with the exception of the White American male, seems to have developed some form of passive resistance suitable to their culture and the conditions under which they are occupied and oppressed. The Irish peasantry developed passive resistance and sabotage of the Protestant landlord class to a fine art, everything from hamstringing prize race horses to burning barns to a whole musical subculture of some of the most rousing and inspiring songs of rebellion and resistance ever to come from the human soul. (Where is the White American's version of "Four Green Fields", one wonders?) The Irish resisted. The Chileans resisted Allende. The Germans resisted Versailles. The British are resisting today. The young people of Eastern Europe are resisting. The Palestinians have resisted the Jews for fifty years. Hell, the blacks in South Africa and the American South resisted the White man in a hundred different ways down through the centuries. **Why do we seem to be the only people** in history faced with an oppression that threatens our very existence, **who seem unable to come up with any kind of resistance?**

This is a subject which clearly is going to require its own special pamphlet or commentary, but I think if you folks consider the situation carefully, you will be able to figure out at least half a dozen ways each day that you can cause the System some kind of grief, and live to fight another day. My favorite kind of "monkeywrenching" has always been to sabotage affirmative action programs in the workplace by making affirmative action employees appear as such obvious incompetent idiots that even Politically Correct management has to do something about it (usually kick the monkoid upstairs), but there are so many other things you can do to monkeywrench the liberal status quo that the mind boggles. I commend to the attention of some of our longer-standing comrades the fabled adventures of the weird, wild, and wonderful denizen of Los Angeles who was dubbed the California Raisin, and some of the bizarre and comic politically incorrect activities he engaged in which were reported in NS Bulletin some years ago.

The Protestant Ethic Strikes Again

The South Carolina lady's second assertion, that I am a failure who should do everyone the kindness of disappearing and ceasing to haunt your feast like Banquo's ghost, is interesting for the "proof" she offers of my failure—specifically, the fact that after many years at the Movement trough I remain miserably poor and broke. I have run across this idea before; it is not an uncommon one in the Movement, but I don't think I have ever analyzed it, and I should do. There is a bearing on the whole situation in which the White race finds itself, as we end a century in disgrace and servitude which we began as undisputed masters of the world.

Some of you may be familiar with something televangelists refer to as "prosperity theology", the idea that if you show your faith in JEEEEZUS by an act of sacrifice (i.e. sending your life's savings to the televangelist) you will be rewarded with divine grace in the form of more material wealth than you donated. The TV preachers who peddle this twaddle usually cite the Biblical verse about casting your bread on the waters, etc. You have probably seen some of the more blatant and crass tub-thumpers reading out letters or introducing idiots with lobotomy grins to their viewers claiming, "Ah sent Brother Hogjowl a thousand dollars outen my kid's college fund to do the work of JEEEE-ZUS, and three weeks later ah won me a brand new Cadillac car in a raffle!"

This is not a new idea. In fact, "prosperity theology" has a long history and entered into the cultural mindset of America from a very early age, beginning with the Puritan settlers of New England. It is sometimes known as the Protestant ethic. Boiled down to essentials and stripped of Biblical salad dressing, the idea is that material wealth is somehow connected to divine grace or approval. The corollaries are that A) the successful acquisition and retention of material wealth is a sign of divine favor and the righteousness of the individual who accumulates that wealth; and B) poverty is therefore a contra-indicator of lacking divine grace and favor, as well as the essentially sinful nature of the person who is poor. Christianity is often referred to as "pie in the sky when you die", but this very strong strain of "prosperity theology" which runs throughout the Protestant segment of the religion is in fact the reverse of that; it maintains that God passes out the milk and cookies here on earth, in this life, to those who deserve them, and that the possession of oodles of this world's goodies signifies righteousness. I seem to recall a verse somewhere about rich men passing a camel through the eye of a needle, but that one seems to have been mislaid by the Brother Hogjowl crew.

True Christianity, love it or hate it, was a faith which our ancestors found entirely compatible with the Aryan racial personality. In "prosperity theology", what we have is the first serious intrusion into traditional Christianity and Western culture of an essentially Jewish principle—the primacy of material things over things of the spirit, or Mammon as true Christians call it. The central idea is that God rewards man for virtue with things, with wealth, and that therefore anyone who has a lot of *things* must be a good guy. Interestingly, one of the foremost public advocates of this concept early in this century was none other than Woodrow Wilson's mentor Bernard Baruch, one of the most powerful Jews who ever lived, so we are able to catch a glimpse of the kosher connection we so seldom see in such matters. In view of the fact that material wealth can be and often is accumulated in ways which are dishonest, cruel, treacherous and disgraceful, the folly of prosperity theology should be obvious. Yet no other idea is so deeply rooted in the American psyche as the belief that poverty equals failure. Ours is a completely materialistic culture; a hundred years of Judaic control of our money and communications and education have ensured that. Now, at the end of this century during the Age of Clinton, the last vestiges of moral standards or principle have been drained away; materialism and its handmaiden, moral relativism, are now about as absolute in this society as they have ever been in human history. We now see *everything* in completely material terms; modern life in Politically Correct America is a cash register and nothing more. When the lady from South Carolina calls me a failure because I am poor, she is entirely correct when viewed by the commonly accepted standards of the late twentieth century, or indeed earlier. Remember, this is America, where poverty, no matter what that poverty's cause, or whether or not (as in my case) it is voluntarily embraced, is viewed as failure.

The Jews Agree, See?

Oddly enough, the lady from South Carolina has some people who agree with her—some Jews from the Simon Wiesenthal Center. They wish I would just shut up and go away, too.

Without going into a long digression on the Usenet madness of the past three years, I need to point out two things. First, we now know that a large number of the approximately 40,000 Hate Harold Usenet posts of the past 3 6 months were the work of a team of about four people whose actual identities are unknown, and who remain hidden behind a series of firewalls, e-mail pseudonyms, anonymous re-mailers and so on. I am not

81

referring to the infamous NA "cyber-cell", whose identities and provenance are known, but to about 50% of the posts which apparently did not come from the NA, were anonymous, and yet which displayed close familiarity with my past and present, specific items of information which obviously came from informers or access to government wiretaps, access to surveillance information during the stalking period of last summer, etc. My money is on the Simon Wiesenthal Center for this because they admitted about eight months ago in one of their internal bulletins that they engage in covert black ops on the Internet against those whom they view as enemies of the Jewish people, and the news media picked up on the story, much to the SWC's chagrin. I can only say that I find the Center's attentions to my humble self flattering. Apparently they have a higher regard for my talents than a lot of our people do.

Secondly, when studying the Hate Harold posts which appear to be of Jewish origin, as opposed to the NA posts which simply scream mindless hatred and threats against me, it is clear that they are organized and that they are following a series of coherent lines or "talking points", trying to plant certain ideas or rumors about me to shape opinion and generally poison the atmosphere around my name, then brewing them into the Internet soup by constant repetition. (For example, for about two months in 1997 there was an entirely serious campaign to accuse me of being the real Unabomber.) This is a fascinating topic (well, to me, anyway, for obvious reasons) but I will manfully resist the temptation to go off on a tangent and simply point out the current Jewish Usenet line on me, since I arrived in Texarkana. Our anonymous kosher internet insects are, in fact, taking the very same line the lady from South Carolina is taking: "Covington is finished; Covington is nothing but an unemployed bum; Covington is broke and doesn't even have a car; ha ha ha look what a miserable failure Covington is, ha ha ho ho don't be a fool don't support this loser," etc. In view of the fact that the Jews themselves invented pure materialism as a substitute for spirituality, it is hardly surprising that they judge my life and work in that manner. Nor, I regret to say, is it really surprising that many Whites do so. The Jews have taught us well, my friends.

Really all I can say in response to this is that I do not believe it is fair or right to judge the worth of a human being based on his ability to obtain and hoard large amounts of material wealth, especially in a society such as ours where personal, moral, and financial corruption have become virtually total.

Yes, there is such a thing as legitimate, bona fide entrepeneurism where a man displays many positive virtues such as industry, thrift, vision, and intelligence in the accumulation of a personal fortune. That kind of entrepeneurship is now almost dead. The current economic system and tax structure and culture have pretty much wiped it out. You still find the odd self-made millionaire, but they are a rarity. The wealthiest people in our society either inherit their wealth, draw it from shares or investments in the institutions of capitalism, or more often they make absolutely obscene amounts of money for manipulating pieces of paper or items of information. Very few wealthy people of today became wealthy through actually producing anything or contributing anything of real value to society.

You're a Mug, Harold

In my case, I have been asked several times over the past two months, sometimes in almost these words, "Harold, why the hell didn't you put some of those donations away for a rainy day, so you wouldn't be in this fix now?" Well, the reason I did not do so is quite simple. Those donations were not given to me for that purpose, and for me to have done anything of the kind would have been stealing. I have made this response on several occasions and been treated to bemused wonder in return. One guy quite seriously responded, "OK, what's your point?"

You see, so utterly corrupt and debased have White Americans become, even those who are racially aware, that we assume everyone else to be just as corrupt and are often genuinely surprised on the rare occasions when we run across someone who is not. Some of you people, apparently, have been giving me your deeply-appreciated financial support over the past five years fully in the expectation that I would steal part of it, and when you found out that I did not the reaction was dubious and disappointed. Some of you evidently feel that you have been backing a mug, a guy who is too dumb to stick his hand into the till when he had a

83

chance. One man told me, in so many words, "Jesus, Harold, you're getting on into middle age and you need to take it where you find it. You should have socked some of those donations away in a little savings account somewhere. Nobody would have known, or cared."

Wrong. *I would have known,* and I would have cared. And the lady from South Carolina is perfectly correct in stating that I am a failure in that sense; I am too dumb to be dishonest in the Age of Clinton, when all is permitted and accepted with apathy by the yawning White blob.

A New Ideal: Holy Aryan Poverty

In the thirteenth century, European culture underwent a crisis of conscience which has some parallels to our present situation. The Church had become totally and irredeemably corrupt and materialistic; immense sums were being squandered on gold furnishings and silk vestments, cardinals' mistresses, and endless squalid intrigue, while the poor were getting screwed without mercy from all sides. One of the reactions to this state of affairs was the rise of a number of movements or tendencies from within the Church, notably the Franciscan Order, who preached what was at that time an utterly revolutionary doctrine: **holy poverty,** based on the life of Christ, the deliberate rejection and renunciation of material wealth.

I don't want to go into a long history lesson here, but the authorities of the time were absolutely appalled. We hear today about St. Francis of Assisi preaching to the birds and the little furries of the forest and all that; what is conveniently forgotten is that St. Francis came within a gnat's hair of being burned at the stake for preaching the heresy of deliberate poverty, and a number of his order were in fact hunted down and murdered by the Church for refusing to belly up to the trough and take their cut from the collection plate. (For those of you who find this period of our racial history in interest, I recommend you read the novel *The Name of the Rose* by Umberto Eco.) No, Harold isn't hearing voices and Harold isn't comparing himself to St. Francis. I have never said I *liked* being poor, but it is something that I accept as a necessary part of my life and something which is essential to the performance of my racial duty. I believe that we need to recognize a concept within the Movement of Holy

84

Aryan Poverty, the deliberate renunciation of the Jew's material goods and the whole way of life which makes us vulnerable to victimization by the power structure.

Anyone who seeks to fight for our Folk must make themselves financially bullet-proof. In the past we have sometimes sought to do this (some of us) by building our own businesses so we do not have an employer, and that works to a certain extent, but not really well. We may be able to accumulate wealth on our own, free of dependence on a corporation or Politically Correct employer, and that's all well and good, but the object is still the accumulation of material wealth rather than adjusting our lives to live with the bare minimum of it, and so when he heat comes on we are still not bullet-proof. Because you see, as long as a White man has something to lose, a house, a car, money in the bank, customers for his business, a family with needs, a wife and children who can be threatened if he steps out of line, then he is really just as helpless in the face of tyranny as if he worked for Shmuckstein International as a Dilbert in a cubicle. **When you have something to lose,** however you got it, **you can be blackmailed into submission** by a threat to your material well being. The only real way to prevent this is by shaping your whole life around your racial duty and adopting a belief system based on spiritual values, be they National Socialist or Christian Identity or whatever, such that material wealth and the things of this world *do not matter.*

One of the reasons the Jews have so carefully trained and conditioned us to be total materialists is so they can have that handle on us, bring us to heel, control our behavior and even our thoughts through their ability to threaten our precious jobs, our money, take away our luxurious homes, the armchair and the television and the endless cold cans of beer we so prize that we become less than men in order to keep it all. From our very birth we are taught by a hundred subliminal methods: Hymie giveth and Hymie can taketh away, so you'd damned well better bless the name of Hymie or else. The Jew has us bound in chains of gold and it is our duty to our people, to ourselves, and to God to break those chains. We must scatter the gold at our feet and trample on it as we walk free and poor into the sunlight.

I have asked you for material wealth in the past as a tool and a

85

weapon to fight for the Fourteen Words, and I will ask you for it again in the future. I see nothing unreasonable about asking you to pass me the ammo. I have never stolen or secreted away one thin dime that you have sent me, and I never will. If that makes me a failure, then I am a failure, and in the words of Rhett Butler, I conclude for the benefit of the lady from South Carolina, "Frankly, madam, I don't give a damn."

Dreaming the Iron Dream

Comrades and Brothers:

As the last summer of this most terrible of centuries begins, I find myself thinking of a day in early summer twenty-eight years ago.

On that day, having completed my last final exam and thus my last day at Chapel Hill High School, I walked up to my car in the parking lot on a hill beside the school. I stopped at the summit of that hill and turned, looking back at the buildings, remembering all that had occurred there over the past three years. In that moment I made a silent vow to myself that I would devote my life to ensuring that someday, no White boy or girl would ever again have to go through what I had to go through in that place.

To my frequent amazement, this vow of mine I have kept through almost three decades of chaos and madness. The century draws to a close and it is not inappropriate, I think, for us as a group to pause for the few remaining months of it and assess where we have all been and what we have done.

Many years ago an author named Norman Spinrad wrote a book called *The Iron Dream*. The book was not a very memorable one, a kind of literary joke, purporting to be what Adolf Hitler would have written had he emigrated to the United States after the Beer Hall Putsch and become a science fiction writer in New York. Yet the phrase has stuck in my mind. I think it is a good one, very descriptive of the kind of vision that National Socialism has for Aryan mankind. National Socialism itself might be said to be an Iron Dream, a vision of a world and a human identity that endures like hard metal instead of decaying like mere flabby flesh, and where the soul of man is hard and strong instead of weak and vacillating. The Iron Dream is the hidden, instinctive soul of our mighty race; it lurks beneath the surface of the mind and desire of every White man and woman ever born, for it is the gift of the God or gods who forged our people from the ice and snow and granite of the vast forested expanse of our ancient homeland.

All my life I have dreamed the Iron Dream. I do not know why; some are simply born out of step with their time, I suppose. Even as a child I understood that things around me weren't *right* somehow, that this was not the way life is supposed to be. Always I have been haunted, obsessed by a vision of a world very different than the one which I grew up in, an all-White world with very different standards and priorities. A world of strength and valor and glory, full of all the qualities and virtues and experiences which have been so deliberately bred out of us by Judaic materialism. When I was young I had an idealized view of the past, all White faces, of course, but I had no idea of what this brave new world should be like in the future, until I discovered and understood the true meaning of Adolf Hitler, the Third Reich and National Socialism.

I have served the Iron Dream since that time, because for me there was no other conceivable path. Every opportunity which presented itself for me to conform (and there were many) I rejected out of hand. It wouldn't have been so hard. Like the ancient Roman emperor Domitian, all the power structure asked was that occasionally, I burn a small pinch of incense on the altars of the false gods of Judaism and materialism. But never once in my life have I burned that small pinch of incense which would have been my ticket into the wonderful world of money and consumer goods—that symbolic gesture of submission which would have meant, among other things, that I would have a medical insurance policy when I reached age forty-five.

At age seventeen, I recognized a racial, moral imperative which demanded my full attention and dedication, and I have submitted to it without question ever since. Not the usual twentieth century life story, to be sure, or at least not a very common one since 1945. "Making my peace with the system", a phrase I have actually heard used in the past few years by some people who were once active in the resistance, is something which simply never occurred to me. I talk about Holy Aryan Poverty, and possibly some of you think I am making a virtue of necessity. I am not. If I had it all to do over again I'd change some things, sure, but I would take essentially the same path I have taken. I have never looked back.

88

Taking Up The Burden

I have spent a large portion of my life making demands on you people—collective, generic "you", those of us who are racially conscious and who know the truth. I am forever asking you to do things that you do not wish to do. In essence I have demanded, and continue to demand, that you come up to my standards. I have done so not in my name, but in the name of the Führer Adolf Hitler and in the name of generations of White children yet unborn, both of whom have the right to demand that sacrifice and that action from you. I have done and said things that have made you extremely uncomfortable. I have spoken aloud of things you feel are better left discreetly unspoken; I have pointed the finger and named names, saying "Thou art the man!" I will continue to do and say these things, because it is my duty to do so, because these things must be done and said and no one else will.

Fraud is the curse of our Movement, more than anything else the cause of fifty years of failure. Let me tell you how to spot a Movement fraud, in one easy lesson. A Movement fraud demands only two things of you: your money and your applause. He never asks you to take any risk; indeed, he would prefer you did not, because if you lose your job you can't contribute money to him, can you? He never asks you to undertake any inconvenience. He never asks you to sacrifice or to endure persecution and pressure and loss and danger for the Aryan race; he convinces you that he will do all these things for you, that the Great Result can be achieved without you yourself assuming any part of the burden which history has placed on our generations of Aryan men and women. In this, the Movement snake oil salesman lies.

Nothing worth having is ever obtained without a struggle and without cost, and everything worth having is always the result of *duty* accepted and fulfilled. The Iron Dream can be made reality—indeed, time and again down through the centuries our people *have* made it a reality— but it requires blood and sweat and gold and tears, prison and death and long years of toil and grinding poverty. Anyone who does not tell you this is lying.

Above all things, National Socialism means *duty*. Duty to one's self, to be true to one's racial destiny. In this soft and supine era most White men run away from duty, will do anything to avoid it, for it is difficult and demanding and interferes with their television. Yet throughout past ages, real men have always embraced duty, sought it out, made it the touchstone of their lives. Man without duty is simply a pig wallowing in a trough, another form of animal life. Man without a higher duty to spiritual principle is no more than a Jew.

To be a National Socialist—to dream the Iron Dream—is to become a servant of history, to take upon oneself the burden of deciding in what form human destiny will be shaped. To be a National Socialist means taking on not only responsibility but moral authority, the right to determine the fate of others, and that is a terrible duty to assume, one which frightens and horrifies most modern men. To be a National Socialist entails the courage to determine that this society is sick beyond saving, and that mercy itself requires its swift extinction. To be a National Socialist requires cultivating the character, the intelligence and the moral strength to recognize the true issues at stake for our race and our civilization in the face of overwhelming public distortion and pressure to conform, and to accept the persecution and the hatred that comes with non-conformity.

National Socialism Vanquishes Fear

One of the first things that struck me at Chapel Hill High, when I began to observe racial reality at first hand, was how *afraid* the White students and teachers were of everything. They were afraid of the niggers physically, but more than that they were afraid of becoming involved, of making moral decisions based on what was right as opposed to what was expedient, afraid of taking a stand in the face of the liberal power structure against the blacks' violence and drugs and their destruction of the learning environment. For the first time I ran into a phenomenon I was to encounter again and again in my adult life: everyone around me knew perfectly well that I was right about the blacks, but no one dared to stand at my side and battle with me against institutional wrongdoing.

White fear has always filled me with shame, for more than anything else, cowardice disgraces our heritage and degrades our Folk. I have striven to show other White people, by the example of my own life, that they can rise above it. I have often thought that one of the reasons that I have always been unable to get any help is not because no one understands what is required, but because most people *do* in fact understand these things, and aside from all other considerations, they are terrified of the responsibility of taking upon themselves the burden of history. The human reality is that most people simply do not have what it takes to be a revolutionary, and that is true in every era. But the fact that most people aren't up to the task doesn't mean that the task need not be done. Racial survival is something we cannot take a pass on. The racial extinction of the White man is not an option. Someone has to step forward, and I have always accepted the fact that, for whatever strange karmic reason, I have drawn the short straw in this life. Sometimes I have wished it wasn't so, but my duty station is assigned and I remain at my post.

The Western world has reached a turning point, by the steep stages of a crisis mounting for generations, a crisis brought on us through our own weakness and cowardice and sloth. Several times throughout this terrible century, in Rhodesia, in South Africa, in the American South, twice in Germany, Aryan man has attempted without success to resist the onslaught of the crawling chaos which is known under so many names— liberalism, socialism, diversity, Political Correctness, multi-culturalism, humanism, all the various nicknames under which Judaic Marxism and its twin brother Judaic capitalism disguise themselves. (Believe it, Marxism is still alive and well in the world today.) We have resisted thus far without success, but that does not mean that we must cease to resist or that those of us who know the truth can ever resign from the struggle. I say to you again, the racial extinction of the White man is not an option, and anyone who accepts it as such to avoid the effort and danger of racial duty damns his immortal soul to hell.

The Honor of Racial Service

We as a people must acquire the will to survive the crisis of civilization, where that will is elsewhere divided, wavering, or absent. At issue is whether our sick and weakened society, which we call Western civilization and which is the sole product of the Aryan race, can in its extremity still call up men and women whose faith in it is so great that they will voluntarily abandon those things which men hold good, including life, to defend it. To be a part of this process, to be a soldier in this world-shaking conflict, is not an onerous thing to be avoided, but an honor, the greatest privilege which can be granted any man or woman, and it is a destiny I would not have missed for the world. The pain that these past twenty-eight years have inflicted upon me is something I cannot even begin to describe to you, but I understood from the very beginning that such pain would be part of the price tag attached to doing my duty, and I accept it without cavil.

Some day you will accept it too, for despite my periodic dressings - down I know full well that you are not bad people, and that you perceive in your hearts that you, as well, have a share in this destiny. However much they may deny it, there persists in every White man and woman a scrap of soul, some faint remnant of conscience. Few White men, no matter how sunk in the fleshpots of Jewish materialism, are so dull as not to understand in at least some part of their consciousness that the crisis exists. It is in fact a total crisis—political, moral, intellectual, religious, social and economic. Nothing more or less is at stake than the continued existence on this earth of people with White skins. You know this, and some day you will join me. This is inevitable, although I make no secret of my hope that it will be sooner rather than later.

Our Race Is Our Nation

National Socialists are bound together not only by a common devotion to our immortal Leader and his ideals, but by a bond of blood which reaches across the barrier of nations, differences of class and education, in defiance of every Jewish rule and tenet: *our race is our nation.* This mighty faith in our own heritage and destiny will some day give us the power to move mountains, and the time will come when at long last we will move men as well. National Socialists are that fragment of Aryan mankind who have recovered our people's long-lost ability to hold convictions and to act upon them, to live, to die, and for our faith.

There is no greater human calling than to sacrifice one's life—either in death or in selfless lifelong devotion, poverty, and obloquy—to an ideal greater than the personal self. This is what National Socialism calls upon Aryan men and women to do. In these times of timidity, prosperity, and inertia this is not a popular message, but a few in every generation respond to it. For idealism is in our very genetic makeup, and however deeply we smother it in the material wealth and indifference of the Judaic world in which we rot, it will always shine through. The spark of the divine essence within our Aryan souls is still there. You feel it yourself, or you would not be reading these lines now.

I know full well that this summer, as occurred to me on that summer day twenty-eight years ago, all across this land there are a small number of young men and women who are looking back at the place where they have just spent some wretchedly miserable years, and they are dedicating their lives to a future where it won't happen again. I have already met some of this new generation and I hope to meet more of them some day, to give them the benefit of my experience and to let them know that they are heirs to the glorious legacy of Hitler and Rockwell. That legacy will come to fruition in the 21st century, and this will happen because a small band of us willingly gave up our places at the great consumer trough, our chances for what Politically Correct society calls happiness, in order to answer the call of our racial duty. It is we who will vindicate our people before the bar of history, we small band of brothers and sisters who gave it all up to do what was right instead of what was convenient or what was socially acceptable. I would not resign my membership in this tiny élite for any price.

It's hell out here, people. It's dirty, it's shabby, it's dangerous, it's depressing, it's hard and brutal. And it is unspeakably glorious. Join me!

Join me! Let us dream the Iron Dream together, that someday the world may awake to that day of blood and fire and renewal which will usher in the greatest Imperium of mankind.

[1999]

Feminists Seize Publishing

I have a couple of interesting personal observations to indicate which vicious little minority seems to be winning the culture wars *within* the left-wing elitist establishment, at least since the Clintons took power.

As some of you know, I also write fiction, and as a kind of hobby I try to market it, mostly to collect and analyze the rejection slips. Needless to say, all my stuff is far too politically incorrect to be published, but some of the responses are suggestive and revealing. The Jews, of course, maintain overall business and financial control of the world publishing industry through the five or six major conglomerates, but what I begin to find fascinating is the editorial aspect of it, where The Agenda is most visible.

My Civil War murder mystery novel has, of course, always been rejected, usually with great frankness by editors who admit that they cannot publish a book with a Confederate hero. (Perhaps significantly, they always say that they *cannot* publish a pro-Southern book, not that they *will not.*) But lately it seems as if the radical feminists have taken over the editorial boards of most publishers. The determination to publish or not has moved away from race to an author's politically correct (or otherwise) treatment of his female fictional characters.

One of the most immediately obvious results of this situation is something that has been noted by a number of literary reviewers and scholars, and that is the virtually total collapse, over the past fifteen years, of science fiction as a literary genre. Most so-called "science fiction" nowadays, as a quick trip down the aisles of your local Waldenbooks or Barnes and Noble looking at the covers will confirm, is actually so-called "science fantasy" involving mythical lands of dragons, elves, magic, and of course all kinds of fetching liberated female characters, witches or space princesses or Xena the Warrior Maiden types who spend the whole book doing down assorted evil males who want to dominate them and make them have babies or some such. (A good example is the last female captain of the Enterprise in the Star Trek cult series; White males have virtually disappeared from Star Trek since its inception 30 years ago.) National Socialists generally being pretty omnivorous readers, I'm sure you will have some idea of the kind of drivel I'm talking about. There simply are no more Robert Heinleins, Ray Bradburys, Brian Aldisses, Philip K. Dicks, or Alfred Besters in sci-fi today. The whole once vital genre has been blanded down and PC'ed and feminized into mush. You can't even get any good old proper sword-and-sorcery fantasy—where is today's equivalent of Robert E. Howard or Clark Ashton Smith or John Norman? The closest we've got is Orson Scott Card, and frankly in my view he is only a pale imitation of earlier s-and-s glories.

A second indicator of the way in which radical feminism has seized control of English-language fiction in all media came to my notice only a few weeks ago. I picked up a paperback copy of a P. D. James murder mystery, *A Mind To Murder*, which was new to me, or so I thought. I was almost thirty pages into the book before I realized that I had actually seen this particular Commander Dalgliesh mystery already dramatized on British television.

Or had I? Because while the names of the characters were the same and the overall plot was the same—a female bureaucrat in a private mental clinic is found done in with a chisel—there were puzzling differences. The television show opened up with Commander Dalgliesh's female partner, a woman detective sergeant, being shot and killed in a warehouse in some unspecified criminal investigation by a man in a ski mask and black jumpsuit; we later learn that this man is a renegade MI5 agent who is covered up for by the evil Conservatives of Britain and sent to a private mental hospital on an island off the coast to "recuperate". There the main murder takes place, and Dalgliesh shows up by helicopter with his new partner, also a "strong woman" copper. There is a whole long digression into the patients at the clinic, which consist of neurotic males, all potential killers, and women who have been driven to nervous breakdowns of various kinds by male persecution. Lunatics are people

95

just like us, don't y'know, mustn't be judgmental and all that rot.

One male patient commits suicide and a second murder is attempted; finally the killer turns out to be a blond, blue-eyed young White man who is a genuine, working artist producing paintings as opposed to the neurotic quasi-Jew pseuds in the clinic. The evil White male MI5 guy also gets his, the female partner of Dalgliesh saves the day, and sisterhood is vindicated.

That's the TV show. The actual P. D. James novel *A Mind To Murder,* written in 1962, bears virtually no resemblance at all to the British television show, circa 1991 or so, I think. In the original book, the clinic is located in the middle of London, not on an island. There is no murder of a female cop by a spook gone berserk. Dalgliesh's partner is the stolid White male Sergeant Martin. There are no pseudo-intellectual psycho patients spouting politically correct drivel; all the suspects in the killing of the administrator are among the staff. Finally, in the book, *the killer is a woman.* The very ending and plot of the novel were altered by television to render the result politically correct.

This is the way these people will rape the fiction of P. D. James, possibly Britain's greatest living mystery writer—and a woman. So I suppose I shouldn't complain about what they've done to *my* work.

* * *

My first encounter with this phenomenon was in my historical novel *Vindictus,* which has as its protagonist a character who must certainly have existed at some stage in real history—the first gunfighter. It's set in the Cromwell period and features a former Royalist soldier who comes home and finds that he's been royally screwed (no pun intended) by his Puritan neighbors who chose the winning side, and he decides to return the favor. I had one female editor reject it on the grounds that my main character, Denzil, "...has a cavalier attitude towards women." Cavalier attitude. Get it? I don't think the silly woman realized the atrocious pun she was making. But the fact is that what she was demanding, essentially, was that I make a character who supposedly existed in the 1650s into a sensitive 90s-kind-of-guy, which is even more absurd. In other words, she wanted me to re-write history, which I won't do.

96

Some time ago I wrote a piece of pure hackwork, a ghost story along the Stephen King line. I won't give the title because I've got another agent nibbling at it at the moment. [2005 note: this became *Revelation 9*.] Without getting overly conceited, I am simply stating a fact when I say that as horror/supernatural stories go, this book is at least as good as 90% of the pure CRAP that is being published in that genre today. This book makes no pretense to be great literature and is chiefly interesting for the fact that it's the only one I have ever written with a female protagonist. About a year ago I had a very strong nibble from an agency, run by women of course, who claimed that they wanted to offer me a contract, but....there just had to be a *few* teensy-weensy changes made....

"Here it comes," I said to myself with a grin, reading their fax. "There's always those few changes." Which I usually won't do because they always want to gut the whole novel, whatever it is, and make it stomach-churningly politically correct. I figured in this case the changes would involve the fact that my heroine, Amy, is a fundamentalist Christian. But no. Explained the head of the agency, I had to rewrite the whole ending of the book, because the female protagonist was perceived by their staff as being "...too much of a victim. Only fiction showing women as strong and independent people in their own right who control their own destinies and triumph over all odds is acceptable in today's market."

The lady didn't say acceptable to whom or why, nor did I ask. The fact that this is a horror story and the protagonist might reasonably be expected to come to a sticky end made no difference at all. Sticky ends in supernatural horror novels are apparently okay for all kinds of White males in the pulp paperbacks, on up to Stephen King's Jack Torrance in *The Shining;* I'm positive if my protagonist had been male there would have been no problem with my book's plot line. But not for les femmes. The fact that the classic of the whole genre, Shirley Jackson's *The Haunting of Hill House,* also has a female protagonist who comes to a sticky end is beside the point, apparently. Shirley Jackson was writing in 1960 under classical Judaic literary Stalinism, before this particular brand of political correctness had set in. It's ironic that Stalinist liberalism controlled by Jewish men of the day actually left American writers with more intellectual freedom than modern-day feminism controlled by

Jewish women; in 1960 so long as you didn't criticize the Soviet Union you had a good chance of being published in New York.

My second encounter with literary feminism was more recent and an even sharper indication of the way the wind is blowing in the halls of the decrepit and PC-riddled publishing industry. After November 1996, I never even bothered to submit my anti-Clinton novel *Fire and Rain* to publishers or agents. We live in a nation of people who re-elected Bill and Hillary Clinton, knowing what they were full well, and there is obviously no point. However, I did try the one agent out in California who did me the favor of pushing my Civil War murder mystery like hell for almost two years, against all the anti-Confederate odds, purely because he liked the book. I came across his address and said, "Eh, what the hell?" I asked him if he wanted to look at *Fire and Rain,* warning him right up front that there was virtually no chance it would ever be published in today's political climate. He read the book, loved it, and sent it back to me in sad agreement. A while later he actually called me on the phone, wanting to know what else I was working on. I ended up half promising to send him a medieval murder mystery I've got about 40,000 words done on, but I doubt I'll ever have time to finish it once the NSWPP HQ gets going. [2005 note: this novel became *The Black Flame.*] We went over all my other stuff, and he said something like, "Pity about *Fire and Rain,*" to which I replied, "Yeah, but I know there's no market for something that's anti-Clinton and exposes the 1960s anti-Vietnam war movement as corrupt, etc."

"No, no," said the agent. "You don't understand. It's not that. If it were only the anti-counterculture and Vietnam stuff I'd at least take a crack at finding you a publisher. No, the problem is Heather."

"Huh?" I asked. Heather is my female lead in *Fire and Rain,* a single mother, Yuppie Barbie doll professional type who starts out very politically correct but gets disenchanted with PC when A) She gets the hots for a handsome Southern detective who is digging into a 26-year-old murder in Chapel Hill; and B) She becomes entangled in the plot and a hit team from the FBI and CIA try to murder her and her daughter in order to cover up the truth about the Vietnam era.

"Heather is a strong, independent woman with all the correct PC credentials at the beginning of the book," explained the literary agent.

"Including your reference to her experimenting with bisexuality like a good PC White female is supposed to do these days. Not only do you have Heather rejecting political correctness with the Vietnam thing, but she also rejects feminism and lesbianism to end up marrying Matt. A conservative, White Southern male more or less rescues a modern 90s career woman from a life of feminism and lesbianism through honorable marriage, commitment, personal courage, and love. That's about as big a no-no as you can possibly commit in today's fiction. If I tried to send that manuscript to some of my editors I'd have a mob of lesbian feminist harpies down from San Francisco on my doorstep tomorrow with pitchforks and torches. They're already suspicious enough of me because of that Civil War novel of yours I tried to peddle, plus some other PI stuff."

There you have it, folks. You wonder why you can't seem to get anything but PC crap on TV and can't seem to find anything but PC crap by way of fiction to read except for stuff written over 30 years ago? This is how it works. The Jews won't put up the money or give an unapproved author the contacts to publish—it's always been like that, of course—but now they don't even have to exert the effort to suppress politically incorrect books. Such material not only doesn't make it past the editor's desk, it never leaves the agent's office, because the agents know full well what will sell and what won't and what will lose them every business contact they have in New York and get them blackballed if they even try to sell it.

"Oh, for a muse of fire ...."

Great Galloping GUBU

Dear Racial Comrades:

Tomorrow is a day of festival all across America, the central feature of which is a turkey. It is of turkeys that I wish to speak.

First, a quick word of explanation. For those of you unfamiliar with the term GUBU, it was invented by Conor Cruise O'Brien in Ireland to describe one of his political enemies, Irish prime minister Charles Haughey. It means Grotesque, Unbelievable, Bizarre, and Unprecedented. The acronym stuck in my head and several years ago I started applying it to the Bad Craziness which comprises 90% of our Movement. For example, Sean Maguire calling Matt Koehl up in the middle of the night to complain that another comrade in the Arlington barracks stole his Cheetos is GUBU. David Duke coming to a rally in North Carolina, taking up a collection in the crowd allegedly to buy himself an airline ticket back to Louisiana, then using the money to purchase cut-rate low-taxed Carolina cigarettes to resell in Louisiana before flying home using the return ticket he had in his pocket all along—that's GUBU. Tom Metzger's ill-fitting toupee is GUBU, as is his habit of screaming out the home addresses of his Movement critics on his telephone message in a clear incitement to criminal violence and nothing at all being done about it by the law.

Willis Carto allowing lunatics to purchase a supplement in Spotlight telling of the coming of the Great Space Alien Ha-Tonn is GUBU. Bo Gritz standing in a cold and deserted parking lot at midnight waiting to meet this space alien because these loons have money they promised to contribute to his political campaign is GUBU. (Actually, what with getting involved in child-custody kidnappings and not being able to shoot straight enough to kill himself, Gritz is a pretty GUBU dude all around.) An individual suing me who claims I libeled him by calling him a mailing list thief, and who then attempts to steal my mailing list through a subpoena duces tecum is GUBU. Buford Furrow bursting into a Jewish day care center in L. A., shooting at cute little kiddies in yarmulkes with an assault rifle, and then taking a taxi to Las Vegas to turn himself in to the FBI is GUBU. The mysterious "suicide" of Benny Klassen was GUBU. Bill Pierce's revolving door harem of East European mail order brides is GUBU. Richard Barrett's ridiculous bib overalls and baseball cap with the little white fuzzball on top are GUBU. Little six and seven man demonstrations wherein we are chased down the street by thousands of Reds and non-white scum are GUBU. The idea that just ignoring all this dysfunctional horse manure will make it go away is GUBU.

You get the idea, I'm sure.

The White racist internet has accelerated the GUBU to previously unknown levels of high weirdness, silly behavior, and just plain nuttiness. Kevin Alfred Strom posting semi-nude beefcake pictures of himself on an allegedly racialist web site. Mysterious e-persons wandering the racist Net signing female names and stirring up every bit of religious and gender-related trouble they can. (One of our correspondents, by the by, seems to have both a male and a female personality and talks to me with both.) The theft of domain names, trademarks, and copyrights for the purpose of smearing and reviling one another. Pornographic web sites paid for with National Alliance membership dues. Periodic outbreaks of usenet hysteria which are literally insane, the posts clearly being the work of people who are sick in their mind; some of you may recall we had two years of that from 1997 to 1998, and it could all start up again tomorrow. Andrew Mathis wagging his nose at us all.

But above all else, internet, thy name is forgery! The first forged e-mail purporting to be from me, complete with faked IP address, headers and routers, appeared in July 1996 about ten days after I first started NSNet. Since then we have seen it all: forged e-mails, forged usenet posts, forged websites bearing stolen domain names containing forged "court documents", forged handles in IRC chat rooms, forged spams to the local rabbi to generate complaints, forged articles allegedly written by me and attempts to plant forged letters in NS Forum. (FTR, I *think* I caught all these in time but in view of recent events they may have managed to slip one or two past me.) As some of you may have gathered, we are in the midst of another outbreak of internet idiocy. I won't go into details except to say that one of our friends from them West Virginny hills has decided he dislikes someone almost as much as me, and he is apparently going around forging this person's name right, left, and center, and claiming in fact to *be* that person. Never mind. It's silly. But I think that this might be a good point for me to re-cap my whole attitude towards this wonderful internet of ours that we are all so fond of. I was just going to re-transmit Claudius's excellent article "Virtual Community", but after some thought I think I need to have another stab at this myself.

Frankly, I have come to the opinion that the Internet is a poisoned chalice. And yes, I am aware of the irony of my using the very Internet I am condemning to make this view known to you. I am also aware of the fact that the genie is out of the bottle and whether I like it or not, the net is here to stay. Nonetheless, I submit for your consideration the following sub-section:

Seven Reasons the Internet is Destroying Our Movement

Reason #1: The internet is too easy.

Any fool can play, and many do. Has anyone besides myself noticed that virtually all physical activity in our so-called Movement has now ceased? No physical effort of any kind is required to peck on a computer keyboard; all is done from a sitting position with the bowl of nachos and the cold beer sitting right beside the PC.

Reason #2: The internet facilitates and enables the accursed *cheapness* which is one of our worst traits.

The net requires only a middling-sized, one-time expenditure for a personal computer and after that, $21.95 per month for an ISP. Nowadays you can even get the ISP for free if you're willing to put up with an ad banner on your screen. We are the products of a totally materialistic Judaic world, and our lust for freebies is apparently insatiable. This phenomenon used to manifest itself in letters I would get from various people explaining to me in abstruse detail why they could not possibly come up with a subscription, but should nonetheless continue to receive my material of the time for free. Now with the internet as the Great Freebie, subscriptions to printed publications have dropped almost to nothing. What have we got left? *Instauration* is gone, *Liberty Bell* is gone, so far as anyone knows Metzger doesn't publish his paper any more and when he does it's just mostly ads for his videos, *Invictus* is gasping and *Truth at Last* and *Spotlight* are on their last legs. How are we going to overthrow this whole evil system when we cannot even persuade the bulk of our own people to part with a few bucks?

Reason #3: The internet liberates our Inner Nut.

Anonymity and distance enable us to behave like the inhabitants of a lunatic asylum in a form of public, while we hide in our dens behind firewalls, Hotmail accounts, web sites, header-stripping anonymous email clients and other devices. When we get on the net we act like Shriners at an out of town convention, getting drunk and chasing the whores and smashing up the hotel in the absence of their wives. Or worse, we let loose the weird demons which seem to lurk in all too many of our minds, with truly GUBU results. Anyone who has ever gotten one of Steve Kendall's vile dev-nulls knows what I mean. Bear in mind that this man is middle aged, married and a father, and holds down a very responsible j ob, but when his fingers touch that keyboard we see that his brain is eaten with worms. That applies to many of the worst offenders in this area; it is very difficult to believe that most of this cyber-nuttiness is the work of men in their forties and fifties. But when we sit down in front of that computer we get a visit from Mr. Hyde.

Anyone who wants to disprove the Lone Wolf theory needs only to look at the demented drivel that spills out of our possessed keyboard fingers. The idea of men like this, who are barely one jump away from hearing voices in their heads, actually overthrowing the most powerful tyranny in human history is palpably absurd. All this neurosis and psychosis needs to be shoved back into the closet. For Christ's sake, some of you guys, turn off the computer, stand up, go to the park and take a walk, go to a ball game or a stock car race, *get a life* in the real world! You may have noticed that my own computer output over the past year has been significantly less that it was in the late 90s; I am learning to ration myself.

103

Reason #4: The internet lets us interact with machines rather than people.

Revolution does not come about solely through communication. It comes about through the co-operative, active effort of human beings working towards a common goal in a given set of real-world conditions. In order to accomplish this, human beings must meet and communicate and interrelate directly with one another, with all the ten thousand and one permutations that human interaction has been prey to since the dawn of time. There is no way around this, but the internet encourages the false idea that there is. On this computer, when I hit these keys to type this sentence, the letters simply appear in compliance to my will. I do not have to send them a long begging letter or make them a complex verbal presentation telling the letters on this screen why they really ought to do their racial duty and appear in the order in which I type them. That's nice. I like working with a machine instead of people myself, and I don't just mean politically. It's so much easier and less stressful, but it will not accomplish my goal. Letters on a computer screen have the power to harm the enemies of my race only insofar as they encourage human beings to commit acts of resistance. Which leads me to:

Reason #5: The internet isn't working.

The internet is politically sterile. It does not produce anything at all in the real world; it produces only more internet. We see a good racist web site and we are inspired—to put up another web site. We get an email from someone we agree with, expressing the nature of our racial problems concisely and with convincing style—and we forward the email to a dozen of our friends who forward it to a dozen of their friends, and while that e-mail is bouncing around in cyberspace Kevin Shifflet is being butchered, Bill Clinton is dropping bombs on White people in Belgrade, and Al Gore is stealing the Presidency of the United States down in Florida by stuffing every ballot box in Miami.

Reason #6: The internet is a two-edged sword.

Sure, we can communicate with one another the world over at the speed of lightning and create web sites with all kinds of pretty pictures. And ZOG can now track us, watch us, monitor our e-mail, slip cookies onto our PCs, archive our Usenet posts, analyze our minds and our feeble efforts at resistance, and spot potential troublemakers. What the hell do you think is behind this business with Alex Curtis? Passing out leaflets and tossing snake skins onto a lawn, a *Federal* case? Bull! The actual acts that Alex Curtis is charged with doing are barely one cut above littering. Alex Curtis is looking at ten years of hard time because the Feds didn't like what he was doing on the internet. How did they know what he was doing? They watched him, and they did it from the comfort of the swivel chairs in their offices. No fisur necessary, no sitting in cars for hours drinking fast food coffee waiting to follow someone around town, probably no electronic eavesdropping necessary. You can tell pretty much what someone is up to nowadays by planting a single cookie on their PC. Occasionally one of us gets silly and actually sends someone rich and powerful a threatening or simply abusive e-mail, and annoys that rich and powerful person. Ever wonder why there's always an arrest in these cases within 24 hours?

Reason #7: We are going to lose the internet.

Yes, I know no one believes this, and I am shouting into the wind here. The fact is that for all its weaknesses, the Jews don't like us having the net. They are trying to create a society where all information and communication flows from the top down. Lateral communication between their wage slaves worries them. Sure, revolt is impossible now, but why take a chance? Things may be different a few years down the road, and when that happens Yehudi doesn't want his pale-skinned servile units communicating with one another; he wants them staring at the tube listening for their master's voice.

By the time of the next election, the White conservative vote will drop below its present 50% and White males will be henceforth permanently outnumbered and outvoted. If the 2000 Nader vote is factored in, we already are. Hillary Clinton will become president. At this point, this country will be transformed into what amounts to a one-party state similar to the PRI in Mexico. The Republicans will remain as the official opposition, but they will have no power and no other opposition parties will be allowed even on paper. Around that time, several things are going to happen to our internet access. Primarily, a legal situation is going to be created where: A) Politically Incorrect ideas will be stigmatized as hatespeech, probably to include any criticism of the Clintons or the Democratic party; B) Internet Service Providers will have their common carrier status revoked and be made legally responsible for whatever they publish or transmit; C) Some kind of legal precedent will be set whereby civil or criminal law can officially connect hatespeech with hatecrime without having to prove actual causality. In other words, in a few years when Buford Furrow goes berserk and they find Richard Kelly Hoskins' book in his van, that in itself will insure the arrest of both Furrow and Hoskins. D) ISPs will be made civilly and criminally liable for hatespeech that allegedly causes hatecrime. They will therefore "police themselves" by driving any ideas even faintly to the right of center off the internet.

When that happens, having lost all our printed publications through cheapness and having become so paranoid we are terrified of giving out mailing addresses, we will be pretty much isolated and totally destroyed. No organized resistance will be possible, and our race will perish. About the year 2020 the White birth rate will fall below the point of no return, and by the year 2100 there will be no White people remaining on this continent under the age of 50. The last White North American will probably die in some remote village in Northern Canada around the year 2130 or so.

* * *

We have an alternative to that terrible fate.

The first thing we need to do is turn off these computers, figuratively speaking. We need to start keeping track of how much time we spend on these machines and then start cutting that time down a little every week. That is what I have been doing for some time. I have gotten myself down to about twenty hours a week now, which for me is good.

Secondly, we need to begin the Northwest Migration in earnest and form actual, physical communities, starting in the dozen or so places mentioned in the Butler Plan. Communities where you don't e-mail your comrades, you talk to them at work or invite them over for dinner, because they live within less than twenty minutes' drive or so from you, not three thousand miles away.

Thirdly, we need to understand that our need is not for communication, but for state power. We need to stop confusing the means with the end. Everything we do must have one purpose: to create a

106

sovereign nation on the face of this earth for White people only. We must *stop doing* anything and everything which does not contribute to this goal, including the infantile forging of other people's names on the internet and the filing of malicious, baseless lawsuits in ZOG's courtrooms against anyone who points out that certain emperors have no clothes. When an emperor has no clothes, the solution is not to try and use force or lies to silence those who remark upon the fact. The solution is for the naked emperor to either clean up his act and get some damned clothes on, or get the hell out of the parade.

This society has developed an almost intolerable **aversion for truth,** and the internet is now being used as a weapon to spread lies by that society. There are those among us who are assisting our rulers in their assorted ongoing acts of deception on the internet, either out of personal greed and petty malice or because they are simply in the pay of the Jews. We know who these people are and yet we do nothing to expose and denounce them. If we are going to use this internet as a tool and a weapon, we must wrestle it away from these people as nearly as such a thing can be done.

I cannot emphasize sufficiently that *we are out of time.* When that jury brought in that unspeakable verdict against a man of 82 and stripped him of everything he owned because he dared to live in this world as a free man, the time for dithering introspection and inaction ran out. We are now officially on the clock, people. We know what we have to do now. Let's do it.

The Song, Not the Singer

Our people are dying. White people throughout the Western world are aging inexorably, our heads growing grayer and our bodies weaker as the years roll on, years in which we have done nothing to stop the slow encroachment of racial death and extinction.

We have fiddled while the Rome we knew burns around us. Every year fewer and fewer White babies are born, to the point where some desperate European countries are at long last offering financial bounties to the dwindling number of young married couples to produce White infants— while at the same time we slaughter millions more through abortion. Every year more and more mud-colored spawn swarm across our open borders, in North America and in Europe. Every year more Whites are butchered like hogs by the blacks and Third Worlders. Their victims are mostly White women, children, and elderly, the very most precious people that any sane society would strive to protect.

The corruption of our government and the loss of our Constitutional rights are now so far advanced that neither can be stopped. In our lifetimes we will see the United States transformed into a Third World tyranny, a de facto one-party oligarchical state like Mexico or Singapore. Racial integration, bureaucratic meddling and political correctness in the public schools have wrought havoc, destroying two whole generations of young White people, turning our sons into illiterate Beavis and Buttheads, and our daughters into air-headed, Clueless Valley Girls who will present us with mulatto grandchildren. We are dying.

For fifty years, a number of us in each generation have understood and fought against the problem. Hundreds of thousands of people down through the past five decades have been involved in a vast spectrum of right-wing and racially oriented attempts to stop the slow coming dark.

108

From John Birchers to Klan to National Socialists and Christian Identity, we have all failed. We have failed wretchedly, miserably, pathetically. Every attempt at organizing a White racial resistance in this country and throughout the English-speaking world has collapsed into a welter of internal bickering, chaos, recrimination, treachery, betrayal, and comic opera incompetence.

Always remember this one key fact: every major right-wing or racial organization in the past fifty years has without exception been destroyed *from within* by its own members, *not* by the government! We are a joke. Our Movement is to real politics what professional wrestling is to real sports—a form of slapstick entertainment.

For twenty-five of those fifty horrible years, I have observed this pathetic Movement from within. I have written article after article, commentary after commentary, arguing, expostulating, ruthlessly exposing those among us who have been, and still are, guilty of the most contemptible crimes and despicable behavior. Over it all I have raised my voice time and time again, arguing, persuading, castigating, pleading, sometimes almost weeping as I have begged my dying people to stop the madness, to think what they are doing, to change their behavior and to return to sanity. I have remained largely unheard, and for all my efforts I have in return been subjected to the most false, vicious and hateful personal smear campaign in the history of American alternative politics. The internet has accelerated this campaign of abuse and defamation against me to levels which have appalled even neutral or liberal observers who do not agree with National Socialism and don't particularly like me. I cannot count the number of emails, letters, and phone calls I have gotten in recent months, sometimes from people who have not spoken to me in years, to the effect of "Harold, this has just gone too far. How in God's name do you stand it?"

I stand it because it is my duty to do so. But there comes a time when one has to sum up a life's vocation, and that time has, I think, come upon me now as far as the Movement goes. This document will be my definitive statement on the Movement—on why it has failed in the past and on what can be done to turn things around, if only we as a people can summon the necessary effort of will to do so.

One final time, I will offer to all of you what I have seen and learned over this past quarter century, as a guide to you who will come after and who will be as horrified, perplexed, and saddened by it all as I have been. I fully understand and accept that once again, I will be largely ignored and shouted down by those who have a vested interest, personal and financial, in maintaining the status quo. But I will have done my duty. You can only lead a horse to water for so long. If he does not want to drink, the time comes when you must let him die. After this I intend to avoid the subject of the Movement as much as possible, or at least as much as I am allowed to do so by the GUBU. The Movement has a tendency to drag one down into the mire no matter how desperately one attempts to break free. But for this one last time, I will try to get through to you. We must change our behavior and our thinking. We are dying.

The Great Paradox

The secret of the Movement's failure for the past fifty years can be summed up in a single sentence. I call it the Covington's Paradox: **"The Cause is so right; the people in it are so wrong."**

Yes, I know I have said this before, but it bears repeating. The Great Paradox must become part of the political and racial thought of our Movement, for without acknowledging and understanding it, our Folk will perish. Our problem is not one of ideology, of tactics, of money, or of propaganda, although all of these have proven woefully deficient. At its very root, our problem is one of people. We simply do not attract and retain the correct caliber of human material to White Right, and until we can correct this problem we will continue to be a grotesque joke. We do not attract and retain mature, responsible adults. We do not attract and retain young people in sufficient numbers. Above all, we do not attract women in any significant numbers. The surest giveaway that something is badly, intrinsically wrong with the Aryan racial nationalist movement is our near total failure to attract any women at all. No human enterprise can hope to succeed with one half of humanity missing from its ranks. I will attempt to explain why the Great Paradox exists, what perpetuates it, and how it can be overcome, and again I must remind you that all of this is based on twenty-five years of first-hand experience. But before I do, let

110

me play devil's advocate with you, as I have often done with myself:

The Jews and the liberals are very much aware of the Great Paradox, and their response down through the years has always been along the lines of: "Your people are all wrong because your cause is wrong; because you oppose and persecute the Apple of God's Eye, the Jews; because you are based only on empty hate; because Jews and non-Whites are really superior to White people and all the history of the past thousand years which looks contrary to that is just a kind of accident which is now being corrected; because destiny has selected the White man for extinction and therefore will only allow you the dregs. You people screw up all the time because you are fools, because you have set yourselves up against the manifest will of God, which is that all human beings will someday be coffee-colored and mostly homosexual, except for the Jewish people who will rule over you forever because we are superior and chosen by God. You don't attract women because you are weak and stupid and ugly and lazy and dysfunctional, poor genetic material, and Nature will not allow you to reproduce. You are *losers!* "

More times than I care to remember, in my despair and my anguish at what I see and hear and experience in our floundering around, I have sat down in the dark night of the soul and gone over it all again in my mind, starting with the proposition "Could it be that the Jews are right? Could it be that they really are God's chosen and we have lethally erred in opposing them? Could it be that it really is part of some inexorable cosmic plan that all of the races of mankind shall be mixed up into a kind of coffee-colored soup, all distinct cultures destroyed and melded into a worldwide consumer society, and that the Aryan should disappear like other extinct species?"

First, I look at the Jews, and without meaning to be blasphemous, I simply say that if they are indeed God's Chosen People, I want no part of a God who would choose a race like this as His representatives on earth. I am not a Christian, but I think the Christians may be onto something when they assert that the Jews are the spawn of Satan. I think it entirely likely that the Jews are in some way psychically or genetically linked with those cosmic forces which are destructive and evil and inimical to human life. Losers we may be, but if the price of becoming a winner is to submit to the implied and oftimes directly stated superiority of these

111

creatures, I do not want to win at such a price.

Then I look at my own people and our incredible, magnificent, unbelievably breath-taking past. I read the words of William Shakespeare. I listen to the sounds of Mozart, of Gregorian chant, the Irish uillean pipes and the bluegrass banjo. I see in my mind's eyes the wooden sailing vessels on which our forefathers crossed the mighty Atlantic, and remember the time I saw a Saturn V lift off from Canaveral. We are the race of the Gothic cathedral, the steam engine and the laser; we are the men who stood in the pass at Thermopylae and charged with Pickett; ours are the sonnets of Petrarch and ours the tongue that all the world now seeks to speak; ours the minds that conceived the very idea of the railroad, the supremacy of law over man, the ideal of freedom itself. We White men, with our sisters at our side, made the world, for good or for ill. Why on earth would the Creator who made and guided us this far cast us aside now? I am one of these people who believe that man was given the rational faculties of the mind in order to use them, and I cannot find any rational, logical reason why my people should perish from the face of the earth just because a loathsome little race of parasites and human serpents hates and envies us. The death of Aryan man is not the will of God, my friends. It is the will of the Jew, and him we can fight. So let's get out of our heads right now any idea that we are wrong to want to save our race, or that we are pre-destined to lose. We are right, and the Jew is wrong, and we can win back our world if we decide to exert the necessary effort of will to do so. Period. End of story.

The Last Real White Men Lived 100 Years Ago

The generation of men born in the Western world during the 1880s and 1890s was the last completely spiritually healthy generation of our race. Every generation since then has been increasingly tainted with Judaism, applying Robert Miles' definition that **Judaism is a state of mind.**

Those who survived the butchery on the Somme and at Verdun gave us Fascism and National Socialism as a kind of moral vaccine, in order that Western man would never go through another such holocaust. They failed, in my opinion because they underestimated the sheer evil of the enemy we face. Theirs was the last generation who truly believed that good must inevitably triumph simply by virtue of being right; sadly, we now know better. Good does not always triumph over evil; if that were true then the Stars and Bars would be flying over my local post office and we'd be reading about National Socialist Germany's Martian colonies in our newspapers. White generations since then have been progressively weaker, flabbier, duller, confused, and poisoned with Judaic values of materialism, ego, and selfishness. It is no surprise that we lack the strength of character our grandfathers and great-grandfathers possessed, and I have come to realize down through the years that it is in fact unrealistic to expect someone raised on MTV to think and behave like a whole, mature man. The entire apparatus of modern Judæo-capitalist society is devoted to denying the White male his manhood and the White woman her womanhood, to reducing us all to economic units of production and consumption devoid of personality, religion, culture, or personal honor. It is no coincidence that the best comrades we now have in the NSWPP are by and large the oldest; they were born into a lost time when moral and ethical standards had not yet completely disappeared, and they still retain some vestiges of Aryan pride, honor and personal integrity.

A Paradox in Three Parts

The Great Paradox is a product of the moral and emotional weakness of post World War Two Aryan man. It has three parts or facets to it, all of which come into play at various times within the Movement.

These weaknesses are intrinsic to the character of the twentieth century White man who has been raised and conditioned to material luxury, high technology, the immediate gratification of all whims and desires, and during a slow erosion of moral standards which is now almost complete. White men born after 1940 are all pretty much amoral. We behave as we do, and not like our brave and honorable ancestors, because we are not spiritually the same men our ancestors were. We are all a product of late twentieth-century America (or Europe), not the generation of one hundred years ago. Our values are largely those of the

113

Jews who shaped and who control the world in which we live. The result is that in our attempts to resist we invariably display the following three character weaknesses:

I. Ego. People enter the Movement for the wrong reasons, seeking to *get something out of it,* not put something *into* it. I have noticed down through the years that virtually everyone who comes into racial political activity brings with them some kind of agenda, be it religious, financial, or political, covert or openly proclaimed—and more often than not, that agenda has little if anything to do with securing the existence of our people and a future for White children.

The overwhelming majority of the weird and dysfunctional behavior commonly manifested by people within the Aryan racialist movement is due in some way to ego, and to these destructive and diversionary personal agendas. Racial people find more often than not that they are working with others who have their own clashing agendas. When these egotists are unable to implement their personal agendas, when they cannot create whatever fantasy world they have decided their Movement involvement must fulfill, they become angry and frustrated and begin lashing out at their leaders and their comrades who are all so stupid and self-centered that they refuse to recognize the urgency and overriding importance of our little personal agenda over theirs. Ambrose Bierce defined an egotist as "A cad and entirely unworthy fellow, who is more interested in himself than in me." He could have been talking about the typical White racist.

Movement people also tend to share another ego-related character defect in common: we either become convinced, or have been convinced from birth, that we are bee's knees. Our ideas are the best, our minds are the most brilliant, our views are the only correct ones, we are totally cool and clever beyond words, we know it all, been there, done that. Anyone so presumptuous as to deny or denigrate what a fine fellow altogether we are, or who is so rude and crude as to hint that we might actually be capable of error—why, such a person is an enemy of the White race! Anyone who so much as suggests that we might make a mistake—blush at the very words! —must of course be an enemy agent! You might call this the Bill Pierce Syndrome; I sometimes think that old codger has *Ich bin Göttlich* embroidered on his underwear.

What we have witnessed over the past fifty years, as time after time our Movement has degenerated into a three-ring circus with a cage full of baboons, is largely the result of trying to put together a working team of people, all of whom have Mount McKinley-sized egos and are convinced that they are bee's knees. The inability of right-wingers, racists and otherwise sincere National Socialists to get along with one another in groups of more than three or four people at a time has become a byword in the Movement; hence the NSWPP's strict adherence to the cell system. Right now, I frankly don't dare get even our group's relatively high quality people together in one room in more than handfuls.

To be fair and complete about this, there is another, slightly more charitable explanation to the question of why we are unable to get along together without squabbling like fishwives, again ego-related. It may legitimately be said that the American Right is the last refuge of the genuine, rugged individualist, the man who marches to the beat of his own drum and makes his stand against all comers, the independent thinker, the true non-conformist, the cracker-barrel philosopher and lone wolf. That, as I have said, is the more charitable explanation, and there is some truth in it. The sad fact is, however, that most of the people who disrupt, destroy, undermine and cause all this ego-related GUBU in the Movement are not independent thinkers or nonconformists. They are assholes. There is a difference: independent thinkers create, while assholes merely destroy.

There is a strong case to be made that the racial enemy is aware of this characteristic of our people and has in the past employed deliberate disrupters—and that they are doing so now, in at least one case, I have no doubt. But we give them a hell of a lot to work with. There's an old saying which cuts to the heart of the Movement's personnel problem: "Great minds talk about ideas; average minds talk about events; little minds talk about people." Most of you reading this will have some Movement experience. What kind of mind comprises the groups you are familiar with?

II. Cowardice. For some reason which defies rational analysis, we have convinced ourselves that there can be such a thing as risk-free revolution.

I know of no other ostensibly revolutionary movement in history, of

115

any kind, who have entered into their struggle with the idea that they would incur no personal risk, and that somehow or other the tyranny they were opposing would simply go away, without any armed forced being applied and without any physical or political struggle. Yet that is apparently what most of our Movement people believe is going to happen as regards the United States government. Apparently, most of us have this touching faith that one day the purity of our ideals will simply overwhelm our enemies, our problems will vanish in a puff of smoke, and the days of Ozzie and Harriet will return.

Our ancestors fought Indians and bears, weathered prairie blizzards, climbed the Rockies and carved homes out of the wilderness. Today, threaten a White man's precious job with some multinational and he crumples like paper. I have witnessed grown men become little short of hysterical when they are exposed to the mildest degree of heat, shrieking to be removed from mailing lists and demanding that the Party never contact them again, ever—and yet these same men would often bitch and moan at me that I wasn't "doing anything" and they wanted "action".

What these people really want, of course, is not action but *entertainment,* which is not the same thing. Anyone in the NSWPP can have all the action they want—but the catch is you have to make it yourself. I cannot comprehend the mindset of someone who embarks on a course aimed at removing and destroying an entire power structure, that of the most powerful and destructive tyranny the world has ever seen, and yet who is genuinely stunned and horrified when that power structure strikes back violently to defend itself. We have this delusion that some tacit understanding exists between ourselves and ZOG, an unspoken agreement that it's all just for laughs, that we won't really do anything to annoy the powers that be and they on their part will kindly refrain from crushing us. Then when the system lashes out and punishes us, we are honestly amazed that they're taking it all seriously. Don't they understand that we don't really mean it? Yes, they do understand that most of us don't really mean it, but sometimes they crush us anyway just to show us who's boss. Ask Randy Weaver.

We scribble and rave in our little cut-and-paste newsletters and shabby tabloids about "Aryan warriors" while declining every opportunity to become a warrior ourselves, even through the gentle warriordom of a computer or through passing out a handful of leaflets. Whenever things get hot in our own Movement, the "Aryan warriors" scurry for cover. Let a few guns go off or let some FBI agents in expensive suits come to our workplace and do Clint Eastwood impressions, and almost without exception our people start screaming "Stop the merry-go-round, I want to get off!"

Sometimes, of course, they find themselves on a roller coaster instead of a merry-go-round. I cannot count the times I have witnessed people get themselves into trouble through their own stupidity and then *blame the Movement* because we cannot provide thousands of dollars for lawyers, and blame the leader (sometimes me, sometimes another; this behavior pattern is universal) because the leader cannot wave a magic wand and make it all go away. When the leader proves unable to pull a rabbit out of a hat, we hear the bleated refrain, "You betrayed me! You got me into trouble!" No, fool, you got *yourself* into trouble because you did something idiotic —just what the devil did you think would happen?

III. Irresponsibility. Another illusion we cherish, even more than the chimera of risk-free revolution, is that of the Man on the White Horse. We long for the mighty leader figure who will descend from the clouds on his snowy steed, waving his shining sword aloft (or possibly his magic wand), and who will do it all for us. We need never incur any personal risk, just write this Man on a White Horse the occasional token donation check, sit back, and applaud while he vanquishes the hordes of ZOG for us. We commit what is, in this degenerate and self-absorbed society, the worst mistake of all—we place our trust in living men instead of in ideas. And the men we trust, almost without exception, turn out to be fatally flawed idols with feet of clay, because this modern world in the main produces only weak and self-centered men. My own feet thus far have not turned clay, but I am amazed and angered and a little frightened by the number of people who seem to see me riding on a White Horse. I of all people know how terribly dangerous that idea is. I have no such steed and make claim to none, I have no magic wand, and I cannot accomplish a damned thing without the active, participatory help of every one of you.

For all practical purposes, the White man worldwide has no leadership, and has not had any since the murder of George Lincoln Rockwell in 1967. There are no actual organizations anywhere on the

White racial right, only individual personalities, sometimes reaching the level of small mail-order businesses with a staff of two or three dogsbodies to fill book orders. The closest thing we have to an organization is still the National Alliance, but their public activity has all but ceased in the past three years as they have devoted themselves completely to selling books over the magical Internet.

William Pierce himself admitted in his October, 1996 NA Bulletin that the entire raison d'être of the NA was to sell books, and all NA activity is now geared towards selling books. They have virtually abandoned the printed word; the last stickers went a year ago and I understand they will not be re-printing *Who Rules America* in hard copy form once those run out. Pierce and the others have discovered the Great White Leader's dream implement, the computer—that versatile tool which allows them to function by interacting with words and machines rather than people. I have been trying desperately to change this situation for the past four years and build the NSWPP up into a genuine organization. I have experienced only limited success, because this would demand intense personal participation from Party supporters and thereby incur some risk of public identification with National Socialism, at which point panic and paranoia sets in and they charge off like lemmings hurling themselves over the cliff.

But at least I *try.* The other Great White Leaders don't even try. They simply pretend to be organizations in order to shake the shekels out of the supporters, their financial livestock. (It is a long recognized Movement truism that the racist couch potatoes kick in more shekels if they think it's going to an organization; actually, all they're doing is supporting the work of one man, be it good or bad, and many of them realize it. They are in a sense paying for a fantasy, an illusion, and the GWLs provide it.) Most Great White Leaders quickly learn to avoid any actual organization or formalized structure, because this involves delegating authority and allowing other people to have access to critical information such as mailing lists, correspondence, financial records, etc. which are the source of the Great White Leader's true power.

How Our Leaders Become Corrupt

The personality of every Great White Leader, almost without exception, becomes corrupted through exposure to the Movement itself and the dysfunctional people in it. By the time the actual sellout occurs, the timbers of his soul have been rotten for a long time. This process can take years, but it seems to be virtually inescapable. Eventually his objective ceases to be racial in nature and becomes personal and economic. The personal goal of almost all Great White Leaders becomes the same: to live without working. Aryan leadership becomes corrupt when, in the mind of the leader, the Movement ceases to be a sacred Cause, and becomes a business.

Of all the Great White leaders of the 1960s and 1970s, Dr. William L. Pierce of the National Alliance is the monarch and exemplar. Pierce is 65 years of age and aside from possibly waiting tables or some such while he was in college, he has never worked a day in his life. From 1965 until the present day, he has lived off the donations and book orders of racially conscious White people. He presently resides on the 345 rolling acres of his West Virginia estate, where he thinks Great Thoughts and diverts himself with a series of Eastern European mail order brides brought to this country with his supporters' funds. His is the standard to which all the others aspire. Matt Koehl, James Warner, Thom Robb, Dan Gayman, and a dozen others are now living out their declining years in modestly comfortable circumstances, having spent their entire adult lives with their snouts in the Movement trough. This process whereby White leadership becomes hopelessly corrupted and compromised is instructive, and I will outline it for you.

Yes, Me Too

Ah, you say, but Harold—what about you? How is it that you have not been corrupted by all this?

The answer is simple. I *have* been corrupted by it all. You can't spend 25 years playing with toxic waste without becoming contaminated to some degree. I have observed these telltale weaknesses in myself as well as in the others. The main difference between me and them is that I recognize these symptoms of Great White Leader syndrome in myself and consciously fight them, more or less successfully thus far, I think—but I still might turn into a Metzger or a Pierce if you folks won't help me stay on the straight and narrow. The others are so self-absorbed that they seem incapable of understanding what has happened to them and probably are genuinely unable to understand that they have been corrupted.

I don't doubt that at least some of their anger against me is genuine and that they honestly believe that my criticisms are false, although I suspect Pierce is capable of sufficient introspection to understand the process whereby he has become a traitor, possibly even deplore it in the privacy of his own thoughts. I hope so; I always admired his work. Robb, Metzger, Koehl, and the lesser mopes? Naaaah. They wouldn't recognize introspection if it walked up and belted them in the mouth.

In The Beginning, Idealism

I have never disputed that people like Thom Robb, Matt Koehl, Tom Metzger, William L. Pierce, and many others were perfectly sincere when they first entered racial politics and were motivated only by the desire to solve the terrible historical problem with which we are faced and create a new and better world. If anyone has even a mediocre level of ability, political instinct, and organizational talent, they can rise in our Movement very rapidly indeed. The trick is simple: say out loud what White people think and believe in their hearts, and they will love you for it. Bingo! Congratulations, you are a leader!

But once you are a Great White Leader you run into two factors which begin the process of your moral and political corruption. First, there is that old bugaboo, *ego.* People write you letters, send you e-mails, call you on the phone and come to your house, all telling you what a fine fellow you are, what a brilliant leader you are, how much they adore you because you say out loud that which they are afraid even to whisper. Like all celebrities, our public personalities attract flatterers and ass-kissers, and since we are all products of twentieth century Judaic materialism, we have not been conditioned from birth to disdain flattery as did our real warrior and pioneer ancestors, to whom flattery was a sign of weakness

120

and dishonesty.

When leaders hear all this stuff about how great they are for long enough, they start believing it. This is compounded if the leader is getting regular media attention. We have been conditioned all our lives to accept television as the ultimate reality and purveyor of truth and celebrity—and if you're constantly on television, and reporters are constantly calling you up and asking you what you think about things, you must be someone special, right? Above the common herd. A Man of Destiny, no less. Since you are a Man of Destiny, you deserve special privileges. You are above the ordinary, run of the mill ethical considerations and obligations that constrain the little guys. Right? You want to tell a lie or pocket some money or stab somebody in the back, it's okay. You're a Man of Destiny, an *übermensch,* and it's all for a greater good. It is in fact your *duty* to tell that lie, steal that money, or betray that former friend. Right?

The first stage of corruption sets in: the Great White Leader comes to identify his own self-interest with the interests of the White racial struggle. He loses whatever prior sense of right and wrong he may have possessed. Like Louis XIV he decides that *"L'etat, c'ést moi."*

The Fatal Attraction

The second corrupting factor is **money in the mail.** One of the great ironies of the Movement is that the very source of life for us, the very wellspring which makes all racial activity possible, is also our greatest cancer.

When someone starts yelling nigger, other White people who have been thinking nigger all their lives but never dared to say it out loud love him for it. One day the newly-minted Great White Leader experiences an epiphany: he opens an envelope and something green and folding falls out. A little light bulb comes on over his head: "Hey, if I can get enough people sending me money in the mail, I won't have to hear that alarm clock go off every morning!" Most of our Great White Leaders aren't much out in the real world. To be sure, Pierce has a physics doctorate, but he is an exception. Don't know what Thom Robb did before he was Exalted, but Virgil Griffin runs a gas station, Metzger repaired TVs, Allen Vincent lived off a government drunk check, Bob Brannen was a

121

janitor, David Duke ran Amway style pyramid schemes, the Trochmanns have a ranch but apparently were living on welfare before the militia thing came along, James Mason was a petty slumlord living off rental property he inherited, and I myself have been everything from a professional soldier to a cab driver to a Dilbert clone in a cubicle. An amazing number of people involved in the Movement in leadership positions have never held any kind of gainful employment at all that anyone knows about.

You can understand why the discovery that people are willing to send these marginal, frustrated failures money in the mail for hollering nigger strikes many of them like a divine revelation. The lure of being able to do something you enjoy for a living, and do it at your own pace, without having to hear that alarm go off at five thirty in the morning and stumble around getting dressed in uncomfortable clothing, then driving through morning rush hour traffic to a job you hate, surrounded by people you despise—to the average Middle American, this is sheer nirvana, and to a real working stiff who has been subsisting on minimum wage labor jobs it becomes the Holy Grail. In a humanly understandable reaction, these men will do anything to achieve full-time Movement status, and they will then do anything—anything at all —to maintain that lifestyle and never have to obtain and hold down real job in the real world again. To achieve full-time Movement is to live the revolutionary fantasy, and it is incredibly exhilarating. They like it. I like it myself.

Before you say it, yes, I and the NSWPP depend on money coming in the mail as well; without it I'd still be a stock clerk in a nursing home like I was in 1977 before I became a Fearless Leader in my own right. The irony of the situation has not escaped me; again, what makes me different is I am aware of the addictive, corrupting effect of money in the mail and I actively set my mind to fight it off. Yet I feel its allure every day. I understand why these men do what they do. But that doesn't make it right.

The Rubicon of Disillusionment

The final step in the corruption of the Great White leader comes when he loses his idealism, i.e. when he finally looks around himself and realizes with a shudder: "These people are never going to *do* anything." It is here that he faces his Rubicon. He is about to give up—and yet he wants to maintain his reality-free lifestyle. He does *not* want to hear that alarm clock at five-thirty in the morning, ever again. How will he do it?

The Great White Leader has come to understand that Middle Americans are not Vikings or frontiersmen. He has come to internalize the knowledge that the people on his mailing list are not the steely-eyed veterans of Verdun and Passchendaele who wore the brown shirt of the SA, nor are they the Confederate army veterans who rode with Forrest and the Klan. He has come to grips with the fact that his mailing list consists mostly of middle-aged men with big bellies and elderly conservatives who send him money so that he will continue to entertain them by crying nigger and by speaking out loud the hate and rage and pain which is in their hearts, but which they dare not speak themselves. The GWL now knows that these people have not the remotest intention of ever *doing* anything that will incur any personal risk on their part, and that if they are backed into a corner they will turn on him and disavow him so fast it will make his head spin, anything to save their jobs and material lifestyle.

The Great White Leader has also come to understand that of the younger people on his mailing list, a small handful have genuine potential and desperately need to be taken in hand, guided and instructed and mentored and motivated—and a larger number have been so badly mentally and emotionally damaged by the filthy society they grew up in that they are dangerous to themselves and others. In short, there will be no revolution, at least not of the kind that will carry him into the White House on the shoulders of a mob shouting "Heil Jones!" or whatever his particular fantasy is.

Let me tell you something, people: every Great White Leader reaches this stage, at some point in his career, and every Great White Leader articulates this situation in his own mind more or less as I have stated above. Matt Koehl went through this. William Pierce went through this. Tom Metzger went through this. Thom Robb went through this. I went through it. Everyone does. The only thing exceptional about me is that I will discuss these things in public, with you. These other men will not, and the fact that I say in public what they dare not utter about our trade is one reason why, among other things, there is now a special website run by the National Alliance for the sole and express purpose of libeling and defaming me.

You give up trying to change the world and substitute racist psychobabble for serious propaganda and political work in the real world with real people. You run away from the real world both physically and politically, going off to some isolated locality where you can breathe fresh country air, think Great Thoughts, and watch that money roll into the post office box down in the little nearby town. But once the rolling acres and the mail-order empire have been achieved, once the Great White Leader has reached the top of the Movement heap, he cannot simply rest on his laurels. Like Pierce, like Metzger, there is no comfortable retirement for him. He must spend the rest of his life fighting off threats to his secluded, comfortable lifestyle. Threats from guys like me who point out in public that the emperor has no clothes, but even more threats from within his own sect from the younger ones who haven't yet lost their idealism and who keep on demanding that the Great White Leader *do* something to justify the money sent to his post office box. That's the problem with pretending to be an organization instead of admitting you're just a mail order book and video company—these pesky idealists who don't get it, who keep demanding that you *do* things, rock the boat in ways that might make the government angry enough to step on you.

So you look for ways to divert people away from the fact that you're just sitting up on your mountain clipping coupons and waiting for those checks in your mail—and that's all you ever have any intention of doing. And one of the ways you can divert your people's attention away from that fact is to dissipate their efforts against soft targets, get them involved in harmless make-work like writing letters to the editor, have a few pointless meetings in rented motel banquet rooms—and sic them on those who dare to criticize and express their skepticism openly. Like Horrible Harold, for instance.

Then the Feds come to you and start making demands, or else they'll start rattling your cage and take away your retirement estate, throwing you out on the street at age 65—and you cut whatever deal they demand, terrified that you will lose it all. And if a Federal building ends up getting

124

blown up and 168 people killed, you cringe and hang on for dear life, hoping it will all just somehow go away.

Can Anything Be Done?

Yes, it can be done. But you have to do it. I can't do it for you.

1. Recover your courage. We have no leaders in part because we have no followers. No real leader is going to waste his time on cowards and poltroons who run for cover at the first breath of heat.

You are of Aryan blood, and valor is part of your genetic makeup, no matter how deeply it has been buried by a lifetime of Judaic conditioning and intimidation. Look into your heart, and make the decision that from this day on you will no longer allow fear to rule your life. To allow fear to rule your life is to disgrace yourself, to be far less than a man, and I want every one of you to stop disgracing yourselves and our Folk. Make the deliberate, conscious decision that your self-respect and your racial duty are more important than your job, your salary, your standing in a community of stupid sheep—and if necessary, your duty and your honor are more important than your relationship with some brainwashed, spiritually dead woman who views you as a meal ticket and nothing more. There are more important things in life than money, material things, and occasional sexual gratification which you must buy with your soul. Our ancestors understood that the things of the spirit matter far, far more than things of the body. We as a race must recover that ideal.

2. Do not tolerate betrayal. Any people who allow themselves to be publicly represented by yellow dogs who make deals with Morris Dees, do real estate and book transactions with Jews, file lawsuits against those who criticize them, commit acts of petty vandalism and defecate on doorsteps—such a people are yellow dogs themselves. Aryans are not dogs, and we will no longer tolerate dogs as our leaders.

We must establish a bottom line below which any person who claims to represent the Aryan race in a leadership capacity is not allowed to sink, and enforce the strictest penalties of financial, political, and personal boycott and ostracism against those who do.

3. Do not tolerate mediocrity. Until we begin demanding only the best from our political and racial leaders, we will continue to get only mediocrity. We get constant mediocrity because we have demonstrated, time and again, that we will allow it to flourish. This has to stop. You have the power to turn this Movement around, the only power that affects these idiots' behavior—the power of the purse. Do not subsidize mediocrity, inaction, or Great White Leaders' private retirement estates. Patronize legitimate book dealers only, men who admit that they are book dealers, rather than Great White Leaders selling books while pretending to be revolutionary organizations. It is time to end the pernicious practice of soliciting money for Aryan revolution and then using it to pay mortgages on large rural estates or legal judgments to Morris Dees

4. Live in the real world. A group needs a headquarters. I agree, we need one as well. Fine, set up a headquarters—down here in the urban lowlands, accessible by interstate and a short run to a major airport, not high on a mountaintop so the leader can hide from people. Do not tolerate any leader who attempts to flee into the hinterlands and sell you books and toys by mail; the revolution will be fought and won where the people are. Wherever feasible, demand that the leader obtain and hold a *job.* I myself have been full time for fifteen months now, and to be frank I wouldn't mind going back to work myself; I understand I need that contact with the real world. That very subject will be on the Party's agenda shortly. Isolation from the real world where people live and work and have to pay bills and raise kids can warp a leader's outlook and make him go funny in the head, and I don't want that happening to me.

5. Kill your ego. Stamp it out. Eradicate it. Surrender forever any idea that you will ever get anything out of the Movement; spend the rest of your life seeking new ways to put something into it. Corny as it sounds, people, I am dead serious about what I am about to say, and it is based on 25 years of experience: The people who get in trouble in this Movement are those—far too many—who enter into this with personal agendas. They crash and burn in a hundred different ways. God will not allow this most holy and sacred cause to be used to advance a personal agenda. On the other hand, it has been my observation that those who enter into this service with a genuinely pure and open heart, selflessly and without a thought for their own egos or their own advantage—those people are sustained and they come through it all by and large unharmed.

The most shining example we have is that of the late Robert Miles: study his life and work and you will understand. It's kind of a Zen thing— like Kane in the Kung Fu television series, we must sacrifice the body to the spirit and "walk the earth". Until it is ours again.

The Disgrace of Racist Funding

The disgrace of racist funding is the fact that, for all practical purposes, there is none.

A number of you over the past several days suggested that I put out a fund appeal to buy the badly needed printer for my computer. I replied regarding the virtual uselessness of putting out any fund appeal in August, and got several replies to the effect of "What do you mean, Harold?" I responded with what my old Movement mentor, Major William Gaedtke of the *real* America First Committee, told me once: "July and August, you might as well pack up and go fishing. Everyone else does."

One of the first things any aspiring young Great White Leader entering the business learns is that right wing and racial fund-raising is *seasonal.* I myself learned from the Money Master himself, Matthias Koehl. I caught him in a professorial mood once at fund-appeal time and he laid it all out for me. "You've got to catch them right about the second week the weather turns in their locality," he told me. "Right when it gets crisp and cool and the leaves get pretty in the fall, early October is the best, and in the spring about the first of April or so. In the spring you want to do a prep for a few weeks as well to try and glom on to their income tax refunds." Koehl actually would watch the weather reports and listen to the short wave meteorological stations to plot the change of season in various locales throughout North America, staggering his mailings of the Fall Building Campaign or Spring Appeal letters to match the cooling or warming.

But after these queries, it occurred to me that we have got an awful lot of new people on our list who have never been treated to one of my candid and embittered tirades on the utter debacle that is Aryan racial funding, so I have decided to give it another whirl. Hang on to your hats and prepare to be dazzled, folks! This is a subject I can really get wound up on. Frank and open discussion of the topic of finance is utterly unknown anywhere else in the Movement; one of the benefits of NSNet is that ole Harold talks about the things none of the other Men of Destiny want you to know about or think about.

But Lord, where to begin, where to begin ?

First off, this is not a fund appeal. It is a discussion of the *topic* of Movement finance. I mention this because you generally find that a "calm discussion of the financial aspect of our wonderful organization" is a fund appeal in disguise. This isn't. Believe me, if I was appealing for money I'd be a hell of a lot more tactful. Most Great White Leaders are terrified to discuss this topic openly, because they are afraid of alienating the financial livestock they regularly harvest in order to keep their mail-order book and toy empires up and running. This is one mirror no one wants to see their reflection in.

Nowhere else in the so-called Movement do the skeletons in our closets rattle more loudly or the unlovely specters at our feast howl more piercingly—our sloth, our selfishness, our cowardice, our greed and egotism. When it comes to money our so-called leaders are as greedy and as dishonest as Shakespeare's Shylock and our so-called "Aryan warriors" are as cheap, as penny-pinching and as selfish as a New England undertaker who saws off the feet of his corpses to make them fit into undersized ready-made coffins. Nowhere else is it more clearly demonstrated that we view the Movement as a game, as entertainment, as a hobby at best, certainly not something one sinks any serious commitment or effort into. Money is *real,* and one does not put money, at least serious money, into a hobby. At least not this hobby.

The first and greatest disgrace of Aryan racial funding is that those who give the most are those who can afford it the least. Anyone who has been involved in the right wing or the Aryan racial movement for any length of time at all can come up with a score of anecdotes about how cheap our "supporters" are, and how generous the poorest and most destitute Whites are when one looks at the proportional aspect of their giving. I cannot count the $20 checks I have received over the years from elderly people living off Social Security, from prisoners' commissary accounts, from teenaged boys and girls who have sent me their allowance, from working men whom I know personally and to whom I know that

129

twenty bucks meant shoes off their childrens' feet and food off their table. And I deeply regret to say that I have also received $20 checks from people who included a note to the effect of, "Dear Harold, I know how important your work for the National Socialist cause is, and I knew I just had to get this to you before I left on my European vacation." Or some similar words to that effect.

And then they fly off to Europe feeling *good* about themselves. That's what gets me!

Then there's the example I cited about a year ago of the guy who gave me a $5 or $10 donation at some really critical time when I had an urgent bill to pay (I can't remember the details), and who does contribute regularly, $5 or $10 a shot. He also lives in a split-level suburban ranch palace. He has two cars and an SUV in his garage. He spends at least $5,000 or more per year on Civil War re-enacting, and he owns several full Confederate infantry and cavalry officers' uniforms, accurate down to the last detail, as well as an armory of functional black powder weapons (including the only working Henry repeater I've ever seen), all of which set him back over ten grand, as he will proudly tell you. The cartridges for the Henry cost something like four bucks a round. The last time I visited his home he merrily challenged me to a chess game using his $276, hand cast Civil War chess set, with pewter pieces—cannon as rooks, cavalrymen as knights, Jefferson Davis and Lincoln as respective blue and gray kings, etc.

I recently had the pleasure of speaking with a long time activist in the Tulsa, Oklahoma area, whom I will not name to spare him the vicious junkyard dog attacks which invariably happen to any Movement figure even suspected of addressing a civil word to me. He described to me his efforts, when he was running for mayor of Tulsa, to get some kind of financial support from a prominent revisionist (whose name some of you might recognize) living in Tulsa—a man who owned three homes and who admits to be worth more than a million dollars. Our candidate finally, literally *got down on his knees* and begged for this man's help. The man gave him a check for fifty dollars and said, "This is a loan. I want it back if you don't win." Movement "cheap bastard-itis" has gotten so bad that even the normally unctuous Ingrid Rimland lost her temper a month or so ago with all her free riders and let them have it, threatening to purge their lazy lurking asses from the Z-Gram list.

Recently I myself had an experience which I want to share with you, because I cannot think of a better example of the problem. There is a man whom I have known for almost twenty years. He is not exactly wealthy, but certainly affluent, a genuine entrepreneur who ran his own business for many years. He is one of those rich men who always displayed a curious trait I've noticed is quite common among affluent racists: they will help a group or leader in kind, i.e. by buying equipment or catering the food and drink at a function, or printing a specific book or pamphlet, sometimes by providing a building, sometimes bailing guys out of jail, but who will almost never actually donate the cash itself, or if they do it's no more than twenty or fifty bucks. This is a common phenomenon and down through the years I've grown used to it. I know it's all we'll ever get out of most of these guys, so I take whatever they offer and say thank you.

This man is also a personal friend. I have visited his home, and he has possibly the finest library of right-wing, racial, and National Socialist books I have ever seen in any private collection except for Ernst Zundel's. I never pushed him about money, partly because one of the things he vaguely promised was that he would leave me all or part of that library in his will, and believe me, books are the way to Harold's heart. (I confess to being an almost obsessive bibliophile, and the way I have been forced to live over the past five years has angered me more than any other reason because I have had to split up the Party library and stash it in various places for safe keeping until such time as the Goat Dance subsides. But I digress.)Anyway, in February of this year—when I was due for a cancer checkup but had no way to afford it and wondering where my rent in the crack house for March was coming from—I got a call from this guy. He told me that he was selling out his share of the business. He anticipated getting around $120,000 for it, net and after taxes.

"Harold," he told me, "You understand that I have family responsibilities and most of this has to go to my children. But I have always hoped that I'd be in a position someday to show my appreciation for everything you've done for our people. I want you to know that I have earmarked part of this for you, and it's definite. You'll be getting a check from me in about two weeks. This money is for you, personally, although I know you will use it mostly for our cause. That's why I'm sending it to you, because you're that kind of guy." Needless to say, I was over the moon; you could have heard my *yes!!!* When I hung up in Dallas. And true to his word, in about two weeks I got a registered letter; I don't mind admitting that my hand trembled when I opened the envelope. And there, by heaven, it lay!

He sent me one hundred dollars.

* * *

People, do you begin to get a glimmer of the kind of thing that I and virtually every other racial leader have gone through? Do you begin to understand one of the many reasons why we have gone nowhere for the past fifty years? What you have to understand is that we are dealing with a *mindset* here, an attitude. You must understand that this man *felt good about himself* for sending me that C-note. He felt that he had done his duty, and I am sure he smoked his Macanudo cigar on his veranda that night filled with deep personal satisfaction. He was one of the good guys, and he had proved it. The idea that he should have tacked a few more zeros onto that check simply never occurred to him.

I was faced with the same options that I, and others who try to carry on the struggle, are always faced with in this situation. Do we press? Do we make a scene? Do we wheedle? Do we tap dance, shuffle, and tug the forelock? Jump through hoops? Do we jump up and down and shit snowballs? Would sarcasm help? Do we pick up the phone or sit down at the word processor and *let this cheap bastard have it,* purely for the blessed satisfaction of it? Do we thereby risk losing what little such a person does contribute? Help that is sometimes timely and on occasion even life-saving? This guy is a very good case in point. Over the years he *has* come through for me in a variety of ways, none of them having to do with money. For example, he has assured me, and I know he means it, that if it ever does come to the point where the homeless shelter yawns before me, I can at least bunk down in his guest room for a time, although how soon I would wear out my welcome is anyone's guess. Should I have risked losing that possible temporary refuge because the man had, entirely unconsciously, pissed in my face?

In the end I simply sent him a polite thank-you note, largely because I

132

was sufficiently familiar with this mindset, in this guy and in others, to know that it was all I could do. To ask one of these affluent closet racists for a check with any serious number of zeros on it is to waste one's breath. For whatever incomprehensible reason, it simply *will not happen,* and I knew it. To these men, the very idea that they should donate actual cash *money,* the real stuff, to what they regard as a hobby would be insane. Had I protested or argued or cajoled this man to give more, he would have regarded me as an ungrateful whelp, a money-grubber, and a heel. Any chance I ever had of getting any help from him ever again would be gone.

Why? How can anyone *not* understand what is needed? How can anyone *not* fulfill this vital duty when one has the ability? I don't know. I honestly don't. I can't understand this thought process; it is alien to me.

* * *

The disgrace of racist funding is that, with the internet, there is no longer any excuse for our Cause being under-financed.

One of the easiest things in the world to do is to accumulate a four-figure electronic mailing list. My own maximum was about 2,500 names a year ago. I am purging and I'm down to about 600 now, and will try to purge down even more. [N.B. - Remember this was written in 1999. - *HAC*] I believe Ingrid Rimland's Z-Gram list at one stage had over 5,000 addies, although she recently purged lurkers.

For argument's sake, let's leave aside the question of how many of these people are Morris Dees spies, government and police monitors, students, Jews of various kinds, idle curiosity seekers, etc. Let's say NSNet—or any other list—has 1,000 names of White people who are genuinely racial in their outlook, who believe in White survival and White power, and who claim to support the racial struggle. Let's say that through some miracle I, or whoever is running the list, can persuade these people to contribute ten dollars per month, the price of a case of cheap domestic beer. That's ten thousand dollars a month, $120,000 per year. Let's further assume that by the same miracle we can persuade these thousand people to kick in an extra $100 per bi-annual fund appeal, in October and on the Führer's birthday in April. Let's be honest, a hundred

133

bucks simply isn't that much money any more, and most people can generally find a hundred for something they really want in the way of consumer goods or toys. That's another $200,000 per year, for a total of $320,000 per annum. *That is a party,* a party created by a mere thousand people, and with no real strain or pain, just the little bit of extra effort that one gives to something that's worth doing.

It's not happening. No one, so far as I know, has even *begun* to make it happen.

Why not? *Why isn't it happening?*

The usual line is that "we want results". (Read entertainment.) But that doesn't make it happen, either. Witness poor Andrew Greenbaum. He did all the things that I have been criticized for not doing. He wore the costume. He leaped in front of the TV cameras at every opportunity and for a while he was the media's official "Mr. Nazi". He called on us to "march in the streets", called for a big rally on public property in the old Rockwell manner (or what we mistakenly believe is the old Rockwell manner). He tried to BE Rockwell, the model we supposedly cherish. He put his own butt on the line. He was a master of the Internet and claimed 1,600 e-contacts, a claim I have no reason at all to question. Of those sixteen hundred, *four people* showed up when the time came to put one's ass where one's mouth had been. In his resignation letter, more significantly he said his group was near bankruptcy, which I can believe. This despite the fact that Andrew also did what I have repeatedly been urged to do to be a "leader", i.e. he sold stuff by mail and on the Internet. And his "supporters" *still* left him hanging out to dry.

The official excuse now being bandied about is that everyone deserted Andrew because he turned out to be a Jew, but that never stopped Benny Klassen, who still has his Buttfuckian Backers six years after he OD'ed in the crapper. Of course, Klassen was a millionaire as well. Our other leaders include a mumbling, vodka-sodden rummy who is paying 50% of his mail order take to Morris Dees; a failed academic whose "inappropriate relationship" (to use a Clintonian term) with certain Federal law enforcement agencies has been the biggest skeleton in our collective closet for years; a Buttfuckian weirdo who still lives with his parents at 28 and who cannot seem to get it through his head that White Americans do not appreciate Jesus Christ being referred to as a dead Jew on a stick; former mental patients who open fire on children in Jewish community centers with semi-autos and then take taxis to Las Vegas to turn themselves in to the FBI; and a bizarre miscellany of very strange and repulsive lesser fry the media occasionally unearth. It is pretty obvious that our standards of character, intelligence, honesty and integrity among our leaders are non-existent. Andrew Greenbaum's failure was not his, it was the Movement's. The kid gave it his best shot, he did all the things we keep saying we want our leaders to do, and he still ended up with egg dripping down his face. We are not a Movement, we are a three-ring circus with a cageful of baboons. This is bad enough, but the fact is that most spectators don't even want to pay the price of admission, they want to sneak in under the tent and watch the clowns and the animal show for free. They don't seem to understand that if they wouldn't be such *cheap bastards* and cough up the price of admission—the price of a case of cheap domestic beer, once a month—the circus might be able to afford to hire some lion tamers and some other decent acts.

This gets into an interesting question. Suppose that somehow we *were* able to trot out a finished product, rather like unveiling a new car in a showroom? All of a sudden *there it is,* a real Aryan revolutionary party with all the basic plant and equipment, the premises, the library, the computer and printing equipment, the staff, the membership kicking in the ten bucks a month and the covert supporters regularly sending in checks with significant numbers of zeros—would things be any different?

We'd have to do quite a bit to sneak it past the Goat Dancers, of course, whose role in the Movement is to try and stop that very thing, nip it in the bud. There would be massive abuse, vilification, slander, lawsuits, harassment, threats, surveillance by private detectives, stolen copyrights and trademarks, and special registered-domain websites directed against the leadership of any such effort on the part of the palefaces to break off the Pierce/Metzger reservation where the Great Kosher Father in Washington has ordered us confined. Can't have us White male savages running off the reservation, now, can we? Very interestingly, poor Andrew Greenbaum got the very same treatment from the very same Goat Dancers as I did. (The "Anti-KOF Resource Center" is run by our old friend Butthead from Daytona.) But suppose we did pull it off and all of a sudden, one day we unveiled a finished product?

135

There would be an initial lemming-like rush to the new party, of course, just as there was a rush to Greenbaum when his KOF first appeared, and a brief rush back to David Duke last winter. But could we make it good? Could we *keep* the ones who rushed to us looking for "action" (read entertainment) and actually get some kind of productivity out of them, if we could move them right into a finished product? I doubt it will happen. ZOG has the Goat Dance drill down pretty good now, and in any case I think we're going to be off the Internet in one way or another in a couple of years. There will come a time when 2,500-name racial listservs and Stormfront will be a thing of the past. But damn, wouldn't it be an interesting experiment if we could pull it off—if somehow we could get that ten bucks a month off these e-mail addies while we've still got them?

Anyway, guys, I'm starting to ramble now, so I'll sign off. I doubt if this has been very enlightening, but Harold does like to have his little rave every now and then.

All Them Naughty Words

I have received a letter today, via snail mail, from one of our elderly gentleman supporters, a man in his eighties who is a long term fan of mine. He has downloaded my recent anti-Clinton novel *Slow Coming Dark* and transferred it to MS Word, and before reading it he did a word search for a number of Anglo-Saxon monosyllables and removed all these ancient but admittedly vulgar and obscene words. He enjoys and appreciates my work, and he enclosed a donation to prove it, but he also gave me a lecture on what he considers my excessive use of what I again concede to be foul language in the book.

I don't mind the scolding. I understand his viewpoint and I also know that he was fortunate enough to grow up in different times when the use of such language indicated that one was stupid, ill bred, a nigger, or all three. I might add that while I am occasionally irritated by the shaking of fingers at me on this topic by people of his generation, I notice that I myself am becoming more and more offended by some of the filthy words and talk I hear in public every day from White kids in their teens and twenties, so it is probably a cumulative generational thing. By the time I am 80 myself, I will probably be writing books as clean as the wind-driven snow and jumping all over other people for letting slip the occasional "damn".

However, I think this is an opportune time to have a few words with most of you who are about to read *Slow Coming Dark,* because this topic leads into another and more serious one: not just the language, but the very presence in the book of two Mafia hoodlums as sort of film noir anti-heroes. I have already gotten one question on this, so let me tackle it now as briefly and succinctly as I can.

* * *

137

First off, a quick thumbnail sketch of the society in which we live. I subtitled *Slow Coming Dark* as "A Novel of the Age of Clinton". What, exactly, is the nature of this age in which we find ourselves? My own answer is that it is an age of open and formalized *moral inversion.*

Every religion, be it Christianity or Buddhism or Confucianism or Islam, or even (in theory) Judaism, has a basic set of certain bedrock moral beliefs in common. These common foundation beliefs are sometimes called the Tao. The Ten Commandments are a good example. Thou Shalt Not Steal (i.e. the institution of private property has divine sanction). Thou Shalt Not Bear False Witness (i.e. truth is an absolute value and worthy in itself.) Thou Shalt Not Commit Adultery (i.e. sex is not purely for pleasure or even reproduction; there are emotional and moral issues and it must be regulated by the community.) Thou Shalt Not Kill/Murder Or At Least Not Kill/Murder Your Own Kind. Another common prohibition is the ban on same-sex perversion, since this is counter-survival and leads to the extinction of the people who practice it. Yet another is the ban on miscegenation, for the same reason.

Okay, this Tao has usually been more honored in the breach. Judaism gets an A for honesty by making it clear in the Talmud that these moral strictures are intended solely for the purpose of keeping the Chosen Ones from robbing one another and cutting each other's throats so that they may more efficiently plunder the *goyim,* and that all non-Jews are fair game for anything from buggery to barratry. But you get the idea. The fact is that there has existed since the dawn of time a fundamental consensus among all human beings that certain things are just plain wrong, and must not be tolerated, much less encouraged, by human society.

One of the most important and significant attributes of liberalism is that it rejects the Tao. Liberalism does not only reject the individual principles, but it is founded on rejection of the very idea that there *are* any such things as fundamental human values of right and wrong at all. For liberalism to flourish, absolutes must be replaced with situation ethics and/ or unlimited shades of gray, with great emphasis on whose ox is being gored. That which has been considered wrong and evil for the past four thousand years of civilization is considered now to be in some cases acceptable and in other cases, laudatory and praiseworthy. What Orwell wrote of in 1984 as double-think is now standard operating procedure in this Age of Clinton.

For example, when Bill Clinton commits sexual perversions in the Oval Office, it is a private matter and in a way even complimentary to Clinton by demonstrating what a stud he is. When Newt Gingrich gets involved in a messy divorce it is a public scandal and disgrace. When someone from the National Alliance (regardless of the cult's actual purpose and agenda) blows up a Federal building, it is a terrible and evil atrocity, but when Janet Reno massacres almost a hundred people, many of them children, in a church, it is an unfortunate mistake and really the fault of the people who were so foolish and misguided as to worship in an unapproved manner. When Hillary Clinton orders the United States military to murder thousands of innocent people in Serbia, it is "liberation". This has all been said before and better by better writers than myself, so I won't labor the point, but I'm sure you get the picture. William Jefferson Blythe Clinton and Hillary Rodham Clinton are not just vicious, incompetent, and amoral. They are *evil,* because they are the conscious agents of a New World Order which seeks to replace the ancient and proven moral values of the Tao with liberal moral relativism and the counter-culture claptrap of "if it feels good, do it." These two people consciously and energetically seek the destruction of Western civilization and the Race that created it.

Christians call them Satanic, and I can dig where they are coming from. I'm not a Christian myself, but I have no difficulty at all in believing that there is some kind of psychic or ritualistic connection between Bill and Hillary Clinton and the cosmic forces which are inimical to human life and human happiness. The revelation some years ago that seances are being conducted in the White House, with the aim of putting Hillary Clinton in touch with the dead spirit of Eleanor Roosevelt and other paranormal entities, is by no means surprising. I would not be at all surprised to learn that the Black Mass itself has been celebrated in the White House since they arrived.

* * *

Okay, so what has this got to do with my two foul-mouthed goombahs in *Slow Coming Dark?* (And, to be sure, the equally foul mouthed Clinton assassins, although at least they are the official villains of the piece?)

Given that we now live in a world which is based on moral inversion, where do we look to resist and counteract that inversion and try to restore truth and moral normalcy? We must seek among the elements which have always existed *outside* acceptable legal and cultural boundaries, and which have therefore been unaffected by the moral rewrite, so to speak. When the institutions of law and order and the apparatus of government are in the hands of criminals; when those institutions are used to exile writers from their homes, ban books, suppress public discussion of the crimes of the Clinton administration, pervert the judicial process into a weapon for personal and political vendettas, kidnap young children for return to Communist dictatorships, and to commit unprecedented acts of corruption and mass murder, then the fabric of human society has broken down to the point where, in essence, the liberals have achieved their goal of destroying all moral standards and all concepts of right and wrong. And since there is no longer any right and wrong in this Age of Clinton, then why should normal people and the Mafia not make common cause? Amorality is in, baby. Everybody's doing it.

"Okay," I hear you geezers and crones mumble, "But why do them Eye-ties have to tawk so dirty?" Because that is the way that Mafia hoodlums talk. The general conversational *oeuvre,* if that is what you want to call it, for the bulk of that dialogue is one I constructed based on published transcripts of the John Gotti wiretaps and electronic surveillance from such establishments as the Ravenite social club in Bensonhurst. It would have been utterly ridiculous for me to make Cosa Nostra bozos discourse like Booth Tarkington characters, or even (shudder at the thought!) try and do an absurdly dated but clean Damon Runyon pastiche. "Guys and Dolls" went out in the 1920s.

One of the things which many readers have noticed about *Slow Coming Dark,* and which they were intended to notice, was the fact that in view of what we have lived through in the past eight years, the overall plot is *not* really that far-fetched at all. The now famous photograph of one of Janet Reno's body-armored gunmen pointing an assault rifle at a six year-old child a few weeks ago was an eerily prescient foreshadowing of certain scenes in my book. I could not possibly have made my many points about the Age of Clinton by making my characters look ridiculous in order to get a "G" rating. We have been making ourselves look ridiculous in various ways for fifty years now, and the result is that we are now living in the Age of Clinton. It has to stop, people. We have to stop fighting hard and start fighting smart, and there are going to be times when, as much as I regret it, we may have to sink beyond the cultural level of Ozzie and Harriet and the Brady Bunch. We live in a world that is half jungle and half sewer, and we are going to have to learn to play by the rules of the jungle and the sewer. We live in a world where all is glitz and marketing and packaging, where the hottest companies to own stock in are utterly worthless dot.coms, and we must learn to market and package and spray on the glitter paint. We must understand and accept that we are no longer trying to erect a solid structure with iron and stone and steel; we are desperately trying to ride out a hurricane by making a primitive shelter of Styrofoam and cereal box tops and Beanie Babies.

There are those of you who have said, "But Harold, should we not try to prove ourselves worthy by setting a higher standard than the Age of Clinton in which we live and give an example of clean living and high thoughts, etc.?" Hoooo, boy, you really opened the door on that one!

I agree completely, yes, we should. I have also made it clear that I think we should start setting such an example in real life, not by talking like Mike and Carol Brady, but by addressing the respective situations which exist regarding the activities and behavior of Tom Metzger and William L. Pierce. I also have to say that I do find it a bit bizarre that my language in a work of fiction bothers some of you, but the fact that we have among us "leaders" who give White racial mail and money to Morris Dees and who do six-figure book and real estate deals with Jews doesn't even appear as a blip on your moral radar screens. But then, "....A *foolish consistency is the hobgoblin of little minds."* [Ralph Waldo Emerson]

You feel I should use my fiction to set an example? Very good. I shall indeed. The example I will set is this: at no point in the future will the copyright to *Slow Coming Dark* ever be sold to any Jewish publishing company. How's that for an example? Certainly it is a badly needed one. Let me simply say that SCD is not meant to be an example of anything. It is meant to be a propaganda weapon against two foul and wicked tyrants, and I hope that it may be of some use along that line. I try to set an example in the way I live my life, and I like to think that every now and

141

then I succeed. Beyond that, I'm usually up to my ass in alligators and I confess, sometimes it is difficult to remember that my original objective was to drain the swamp.

I don't like it any more than you do, folks. Some of you may recall that in the back of the Recommended Reading List I put my own personal picks, prominent among which were the works of Arthur Conan Doyle, Booth Tarkington, and H. P. Lovecraft. So far as I can recall, with one breathless and, for 1914, very daring exception in Tarkington's "Seventeen", there is not even a single "damn" in the pejorative sense. That's a large part of what I read for my own pleasure and relaxation, and I hope it tells you something about me. I would give my eye teeth to have been born into the world that some of you octogenarians knew when you were young, but I was not. We are living in the Age of Clinton. And *Slow Coming Dark* is a novel of that age.

Defeating the Hidden Hand

Of the many objections raised against the Northwest migration, few have any real validity when placed alongside the long term reality that we are going to become extinct as a people if we don't quit pecking on keyboards and act. However, there is one valid and important question which we must face up to and plan to overcome. That question is: in view of the fact that we have made a complete hash-up of every racial resistance project that we have undertaken for the past half a century, what guarantee is there that we will not make a similar dog's dinner of it in the Northwest? The obvious corollary is that if we are going to fail again, why not fail in our own homes?

This problem is serious but not insoluble. The difficulty is that in order to insure that we don't cock it up in this, our long awaited main event, the Movement must proceed with a clear, accurate, self deception-free understanding of exactly why we have been failing all these years to begin with. You can't fix something until you know what's wrong with it. Thus far our track record on fearless and favorless self-analysis, along with internal correction of our own errors, has been somewhat less than impressive. For many years the urgent imperative for reform within our own ranks has been made clear with overwhelming force by a series of events which have ranged from the merely GUBU to the downright catastrophic. I am quite frankly astounded that we have survived even in our present sickly and moribund form, considering the steady diet of political junk food and snake oil we have been consuming and the number of times we have allowed ourselves to be seduced, abused and abandoned by a series of charming and not so charming cads. They say the good Lord looks out for drunkards, fools, and children, and we are the living proof of that ancient aphorism. Mere luck doesn't explain our survival, that much is certain.

143

I have said it before and I will say it again: the most important obstacle to White racial survival is our own character, or lack thereof. Virtually every other aspect of this situation revolves around the character issue. When White males become White men again, the bulk of our problems will be solved. However, there is something else that I believe it is time we discussed, and that is how, exactly, the external enemy (as opposed to the one we see in the mirror every morning) has taken advantage of our clearly perceived weaknesses to make sure that not once in the past fifty years have we managed to get past square one.

The repulsive Franklin Delano Roosevelt once wrote that "In politics, nothing ever happens accidentally," while on the opposite end of the spectrum, Bismarck said "An inability to believe in conspiracies is the true mark of the liberal." And Bismarck knew about such things. Both men knew whereof they spoke. Yes, Virginia, human beings do conspire, and **just because you're paranoid, that don't mean they ain't out to get you. Paranoids have enemies too.** While we have brought most of our failure upon ourselves through weakness and cowardice and sloth and stupidity, it cannot be denied that at times we have been provided with an outside assist. There is no question that once ZOG recognizes we are serious about the Northwest (and we are), the same tactics which have been used against us in the past will be deployed again in spades, including in some cases through the very same people.

We have all wondered in the past "how it really works," how the System has kept our people down and kept itself in power in the teeth of policies and behavior that virtually shout from the rooftop our rulers' intention to kill us all. In almost any other country in the world, a government and a ruling class that comported itself in the manner of ours would have been overthrown long ago and the guillotine would have slaked its thirst with blue and kosher blood. Even in the Soviet Union, eventually people got a bellyful of the Bolsheviks. So here is my own personal take on how this little game really works.

The Hidden Hand

It is my belief that ever since 1945, and possibly before that, there has existed within the highest echelons of the American ruling élite a kind of movement or conspiracy to maintain the present Anglo-Zionist international, financial power structure and to make sure that White, Christian or otherwise Western males never mount any kind of effective resistance to the Agenda, or progressive humanism, or liberal democracy, or whatever you want to call the consensus-based belief system that all religions and cultures must be destroyed and the races of mankind must be melded into one single coffee-colored mass. In deference to the Ghost of Right Wing Paranoia Past, I call this shadowy enterprise The Hidden Hand.

We are speaking here of something dim and vague and amorphous, ill-defined and constantly changing in shape and scope. The late Rev. Robert Miles defined Judaism as a state of mind, one of the most profound analyses I have ever heard. Just as National Socialism is the soul of our Folk expressed in mortally comprehensible thoughts and words, so our enemy is basically an idea that occasionally assumes definable human shape. The Hidden Hand is Jewish, but the Hidden Hand is also impeccably WASP dressed in a banker's suit. Both the Jew and the wealthy White capitalist have clear interests in maintaining the present liberal democratic status quo, and they routinely work together despite their personal antipathies. The Hidden Hand is ADL, it is FBI, it is CB S, it is sometimes all three at once. For example, I have always been convinced, for reasons I won't get into here, that my old buddy Special Agent Richard Goldberg on more than one occasion wore his ADL hat instead of his FBI hat when he was engaged in certain activities. While in every decade there have been certain key men involved in various projects and operations of the Hidden Hand, all designed to deprive White men of their rights and their country and eventually of their existence as a race, I suspect that even these key men could not give an accurate accounting of their conspiracy's exact nature, strength, and activities at any given moment. There are many left Hands and many right Hands, and few of them know what the others do.

I do not believe that there is any one particular group or organization charged with keeping the White man supine and in his place. There is no "Bureau of Honky Repression" as such, although several Federal agencies such as the FBI and BATF have come close at times. I may be wrong, but if I am then formal organization and self-awareness of this Hidden Hand is a very recent development. I think that like the liberal movement itself, this covert effort is based on consensus and loose alliance towards a common purpose on the part of many disparate elements of the Establishment. I am fairly sure that under the Clintons this general tendency has become far more formalized than it has been in the past and may indeed now have such things as offices, staff, and a budget somewhere within the bowels of the bureaucracy, in some high-security sub-basement in the Department of Agriculture labeled "Statistics" or something of the kind. If so, we will never know. Government, police and Federal law enforcement, media, left-wing monitoring groups, organized churches, big business and the local Chamber of Commerce, covert homosexuals working behind the scene from positions of power and influence where even today admitting their perverse sexual orientation would be unwise, all of these take their turn at bat for the Hidden Hand as required. One Hidden Hand washes the other and scratches the other's back in any case where it is understood among those in power that something White and dangerous must be suppressed, discredited, undermined or destroyed.

Certain elements of the Hand do have a known role in things. The ADL, for example, gathers intelligence on anything and anyone to the right of center, concentrating on critics of Israel and anyone who entertains, or is suspected to entertain unapproved thoughts regarding the historical role and the desirability of the Jewish people. They are supplemented these days by various leftist monitoring groups who perform the same function on behalf of "persons of color", spying on any White group or individual who is suspected of welcoming the incoming hordes of brown-skinned foreigners who are overrunning North America with less than open arms. The FBI and BATF persecute, torture, and arrest. The judges pass crushing sentences of amazing cruelty for passing out a few leaflets or punching some scumbag with a brown skin. The media create a tissue of lies and slanders against individual White men and Hollywood insults and denigrates and ridicules our entire race; Homer Simpson is the classic case of the Hidden Hand in media.

The Hidden Hand in Action

We will leave aside for the moment some of the more obvious things like FBI and BATF raids and stings, the recent arrest of Alex Curtis, etc. These things are not true Hidden hand operations, they are politically motivated pre-emptive strikes undertaken by specific people in Federal law enforcement at the behest of specific agencies who are beginning to feel nervous about a given individual or group, or who feel that there is political capital to be made from being perceived as "tough on racism" by the liberal democratic establishment. More importantly, incidents such as the Alex Curtis affair are done openly. They are helpful to the Hidden Hand, but not of it. The true Hidden Hand is far more shadowy and operates in the background; almost never do we perceive any provable evidence of its existence, never mind being able to trace a certain event or rumor or situation to its source. (Cue the theme music from *The X Files.*) Okay, I know all of this sounds melodramatic, but Count Bismarck was right. People do conspire, and people in power conspire quite a lot.

What does the Hidden Hand actually *do,* other than spy on us and use their media to tell lies about us? Here is where we venture onto ground where all of us chickens start getting uncomfortable, because it leads towards certain subjects which we have conditioned ourselves to avoid thinking about. I must word this very carefully, because already I can see your fingers raising towards your ears and your eyes getting ready to squinch tightly shut lest you hear or see anything which might cause you inadvertently to think painful thoughts.

To come to the point, it is my belief that for the past fifty years, this mysterious and barely perceived Hidden Hand has not restricted itself only to deliberate and organized efforts to monitor us, i.e. spy on us and turn what they find out over to the police so they can arrest and torture and imprison us. Nor have these powerful and covert enemies confined themselves to public relations, i.e. anti-White propaganda in the media and the entertainment industry. It is my belief that this obscure and half-perceived tendency, acting sometimes through the government but more often through private vigilante groups like the ADL, has conducted regular infiltration exercises with the purpose of disruption of all our efforts. I believe that periodically this conspiracy has inserted into our

147

ranks highly skilled, paid agents provocateur, agents intensively trained in psychological techniques of disruption, suggestion, manipulation, and organizational sabotage. In other words, it's not just our people acting like idiots, it's deliberate.

I believe that these men (and occasionally women) are not placed among us simply for a few months and withdrawn. The Hidden Hand thinks in the long term and meticulously plans decades in advance.

I believe that these people are highly dedicated professionals, mercenary political operatives who stay among us for many years at a time, usually moving from group to group and locality to locality but sometimes functioning as "sleepers," staying in one place and building up whole false personae and histories to give them credibility.

I believe that there are men among us, even today, who pretend to believe in our cause but who are wearing a mask, while covert numbered bank accounts swell each month with large salary checks drawn on anonymous accounts in the Cayman Islands or something of the kind. It is furthermore my belief—no, damn you, keep those fingers out of your ears!—it is furthermore my belief that with clear-headed observation and a willingness to use our minds objectively, these men may be identified with virtual certainty through a recognizable pattern in their *observed behavior.*

I believe that whenever a man, who is clearly of sufficient intelligence to understand what he is doing, repeatedly behaves in such a manner as to destroy and undermine multiple White resistance efforts and to give aid and comfort to the enemy, it is neither unwise nor unreasonable publicly to question his actions and his motives, since we currently have no mechanism or ability to question these men privately in the appropriate manner.

No, open those eyes and get those fingers out of your ears!

All right, all right! I promise I will not utter The Forbidden Name, He Who Is So Great And Wonderful That He Is Beyond All Question Or Doubt No Matter What He Does. I am trying to make sure that the Northwest Imperative doesn't fizzle like everything else we've done for the past fifty years. In order to accomplish that you've got to listen and your mind mustn't snap shut, so however reluctantly, I promise you I won't allow The Forbidden Name to pass my blasphemous lips. Happy

148

now? That proviso agreed, an example from real life is certainly in order. I won't name the individual, lest I defame, and horror of horrors, we wouldn't want that, now, would we? Besides, at the moment I'm not pointing a finger, I'm trying to make a point, if you get the difference. I am describing this person as a phenomenon, as a piece of evidence, rather than as an indictment, so in that context his name isn't important. Let's take a look at a very real Movement career.

About fourteen years ago, this man appears on the Movement scene. No one knows where he comes from, and he has told various stories about his past to different people at different times which conflict and contradict one another. Little things like not being able to get his age straight, for example. The conflicts aren't really major, and you have to meet people who have known him down through the years and pick their brains of everything he told them and everything they have observed about him, but when you put the bits and pieces from the last fourteen years together, you notice a whole series of small but odd inconsistencies, like a job applicant hasn't quite memorized his own doctored resume.

This man has never held down a job or had any visible means of support, not in fourteen years, although he always has some good line or other as to why he has money. Another very odd thing I have only recently been able to document, although I'd heard it before, is this. At certain times in his career—not always, this comes and goes—he goes through periods where about once every month or six weeks, he disappears for about ten days at a time and no one really knows where he goes or what he does. He claims he is doing some job involving travel and that's how he comes to have money all the time, but there's never any substantiation for this and no one ever seems to be able to contact him or trace his movements during these periodic absences.

In the past fourteen years this man has been actively involved in nine White racial groups. Six of these orgs no longer exist, two of them are in a staggering shambles now, and the only one which may be fairly said to be still going strong is one where his involvement was only peripheral and where circumstances did not allow him to ease his way into a position on the right hand of the group leader.

This man goes where the action is, and all of a sudden in a matter of months, there's where the action *isn't*. He does nothing overt. He is

149

smooth and plausible, especially at first when he is flattering and worming his way close in, right next to the leader of the group. He is helpful. He has a certain degree of talent and ability and he claims to have much more. After a while, people begin to notice that every project he undertakes for his latest racial group turns into an unmitigated fiasco, costing time and money and generating negative publicity and in several cases jail sentences for people involved. But he always has an answer, always a plausible explanation, that explanation being how it was all really someone else's fault.

After a while the entire group suddenly collapses into a welter of backstabbing, wild accusations and angry recriminations, "open letters" and dissension and general GUBU. People leave the group in droves. Operations shrink and then cease altogether, publications fold for lack of funds, splinter groups break away in a desperate attempt to re-establish what was lost free of this man's baleful and destructive aura. There are mysterious deaths which are never quite fully explained to everyone's satisfaction. Large sums of money and valuable group assets disappear or find their way into hands where they clearly do not belong. The group becomes a hollow shell of what it was. Once it has been drained of vitality and people and direction and substance, this man moves on to the next racial group—and with his usual plausibility and initial eagerness for "the Cause", he always finds a taker.

I have studied his career with no little awe as the years have gone by. He has moved through our little Movement like the Grim Reaper, sowing dissension, collapse, and chaos wherever he goes. He has accounted for more permanent manpower losses to the racial right through disgusted resignation and other forms of elimination than a hundred FBI investigations or Morris Dees lawsuits, and he stands now on the verge of his greatest act of political devastation yet, an act which I have to say he will probably accomplish.

There is a small coterie of people who swear by this man, who would trust him with their lives, who would swear any oath and take any risk that he is really and truly one of us—and a not so small army of other people down through the years who hate him like a loathsome serpent and who will never have anything more to do with any White cause because of what they experienced at this man's instigation. I assert without hesitation that this man is the greatest asset which the Jewish people and their power structure currently possess in their struggle to suppress Aryan dissent. The question is: are we to believe that this man and his activities for the past fourteen years are accidental?

And there are others. I have identified about half a dozen people within our Movement whom I have known over the past 25 years whose behavior was and is so suspicious to me, so clearly counterproductive, negative and destructive to the cause that they purport to believe in and work for, that I simply cannot rid myself of the suspicion that they have done these things deliberately. Three of them are still active besides the individual I spoke of previously. I am not talking about obvious ATF agents like Bernard Butkovich or obvious lunatics like Jackson Grimes. Nor am I talking about Tom Metzger or Dr. William Pierce and a few others who started out sincere, let money distract them from the task at hand, and later became discouraged and finally corrupt. (Sorry, I just couldn't resist.) I am talking about a carefully planned, deliberate, well financed, long term scheme on the part of the Jews and the establishment they have created to ensure that we go nowhere—without the necessity of them engaging in blatant disregard of the Constitution.

The ideal status quo which the Jews have always aimed at is one where appearances are maintained, where we can exist and thus maintain the pretense that we have freedom and rights, but where we are unable effectively to exercise those rights. In other words, **"You may exist, but you may not function."** We can live, but only in a straitjacket. We may speak, but the minute we begin to be heard (as on the Internet) bad things will mysteriously begin to happen, things seemingly unconnected to anything outside but which appear to come from within. The phrase "South Lebanon Army" irresistibly suggests itself in this context.

Whenever anyone reaches a certain level of effectiveness in the Movement, it is like "someone threw a switch". I have heard that expression used dozens of times down through the years by people separated by time and distance in every group from Klan to Identity. It has happened to Maynard Campbell, George Burdi, Gary Gallo, Wolf Droege, Al Baron, Charlie Sargent, Bob White of the Duck Club, J. B. Stoner, Willis Carto, Dewey Tucker, Glenn Miller, James Wickstrom, and a score of others whom you have probably never heard of. There is a reason why you have never heard of them. Someone made darn sure you didn't. It's been done to David Duke a couple of times but he's bounced back. It was tried on Dr. Ed Fields back in 1984, but he survived.

In my case, it happened in 1981 with the NSPA where I found the rug pulled neatly out from under me and five years' worth of work destroyed in a matter of weeks by people whom I would have trusted with my life. In that case I believe now, after years of reflection and replay in my own mind, that I know what happened. One man whom I believe to have been one of these disrupters I speak of came into the organization, wormed his way in too close (my fault, for which I accept full responsibility), spotted the one individual in our team with too much ambition, too much love of money, and with serious emotional and personality problems, and very adeptly triggered the whole thing with a handful of letters, phone calls, and surreptitious meetings in an IHOP on Hillsborough Street. I've seen a master craftsman in action, I'll say that. It took him six months to set the whole thing up, but once he had it all in place the Party of that day came down like one of those imploded buildings you see on the news.

How the Hidden Hand Will Attempt To Undermine the Northwest Migration

OK, on to more modern material. Based on past experience, here is what I think we will run up against in the Northwest.

We will leave aside the expected problems with actual police and Federal thugs. About all we can do to keep those off our back is make sure we don't break the law and make it hard for them to fabricate anything against the Incomers. I am speaking now of the Hidden Hand that operates at enemy direction from within our ranks. At the moment we are in a kind of lull because the people who control the Hand don't yet fully understand that we are serious. The attitude seems to be, "Oh, Harold is just going through a phase and it will wear off after the holidays, then they'll be back to simply pecking at keyboards and going around and around and around while getting nowhere." I figure about January or February they are going to wake up, it will hit them that we're serious and that there is in fact the beginning here of a serious threat to the status quo. So expect the following:

152

Dissing the Idea. Expect a number of public attacks on the whole idea of going Northwest, and on the Homeland itself. It is impractical. "The government would never let us do it" (neatly avoiding the question of just what *will* the government let us do?) You won't be able to get a job there. Everything is too expensive or too primitive or too different. The Northwest is full of horrible brainwashed liberal White people who will not strew flowers at our feet as we roll into town and so we mustn't do it. The weather is so cold in winter, etc. Doom, doom and gloom! A hundred different petty reasons will be dreamed up not to go, all tending towards the same conclusion: we must do nothing but sit and wait and peck on keyboards until "something comes up."

Of course, something *has* come up—the ideal of the Homeland. And that is what will be getting these hornets buzzing.

Let me make something clear here. I'm not saying that everyone who opposes the Northwest Migration is working for the Hidden Hand. Nor will it all be ill intentioned. Some of this is going to come from our own Movement Eeyores who simply rubbish every idea that anyone comes up with. Some of it will come from people who are genuinely unable to come to grips with the increasingly clear handwriting on the wall that we will now never be able to seize back all of our country at once and magically bring back the days of Mom, apple pie, and the Beaver. Natural and principled opposition to the Northwest Migration will always be present, although as the years roll by and the situation becomes increasingly stark, this opposition will eventually melt away in the face of reality.

But look for patterns in distribution here. When doom and gloom appears in NS Forum, that's one thing. I put it there, usually to answer it. When anti-Northwest doom and gloom starts getting e-mailed all over the Internet and dropping into racial people's mailboxes in newsletter form, take a good sharp look at who wrote it and why. Five will get you ten that it comes from He Who May Not Be Named Lest You Stuff Your Fingers In Your Ears And Squinch Your Eyes Shut, Count Stolichnaya down in San Diego, a certain fruitfly in Mississippi—or else it's wholly or quasi-anonymous, signed with some name you never heard of. This Movement is shrinking and we all pretty much know one another. Any time that something is not traceable to a known source—you can pretty well

153

assume that you know the source.

Dissing Your Friend and humble Gensec. Expect personal attacks on me to resume at full spate, both printed and Internet. I will of course become The Hidden Hand myself, conspiring to get everybody to waste time moving to Idaho at the behest of my evil Jewish masters. Don't
worry, I'm already starting to pick up on that one and it doesn't bother me. It's expected. Call it an intelligence test; anyone dumb enough to believe it, we don't need. I long ago gave up trying to prove anything about myself to anyone. Read what I write and make your own decision.

A Rival Plan. At some point, once they realize that the Northwest Idea isn't dying out, the Hand will try the old bait and switch. Movement people have the attention span of a housefly, as do pretty much all Middle Americans, and that they are always ready to gape and gawp at the newest
dude up on the wagon platform selling snake oil at a dollar a bottle. They will provide us with said dude and said snake oil. Most likely, what we will
be served up with is a new Great White Leader who promises that he will do it all for us, while we sit in the comfort of our armchairs and go ooooh!
aaaaah! For such a mission I don't think we'll see any costumes—this one will be important for their agenda. No, with our new Great White Leader to come, look for sharp three-piece suits and photogenic good looks. Kind of a David Duke without all the baggage, a telegenic Great White Hope in whose charismatic hands we can leave our racial destiny and relax. And of course, forget about all this Northwest nonsense.

Mark my words, people—in another year or two, such a man will appear on the political horizon. Observe him, support him if you want—but do it from Spokane or Portland or Bremerton, not the Rust Belt.

Unleash the Looney Tunes. I will believe to my dying day that the disruption and destruction of Jost Turner's little National Socialist community in the California mountains was done deliberately. A certain Induhvidual and several companions with impeccable "NS" credentials wormed their way into residence and very soon afterwards were goose-stepping around town in White Power T-shirts with Doc Marten boots and

154

shaven heads, waving beer cans in the air and screaming "White Power!", assaulting the locals and vandalizing their property and generally acting like escapees from the cackle box. In short order a dozen years' worth of careful, painstaking community relations that Jost had built up with his local neighbors went down the tubes. I have often wondered how much of a part pure anger and chagrin played in the heart attack that killed Jost.

As our communities in the Northwest begin to take shape, there will appear among us strange little men who do strange things. Judging by some of the things the Hidden Hand threw at the Aryan Nations, this could get very nasty indeed, including big, bad racist types who are suddenly and mysteriously exposed to have criminal records for child molestation and that kind of thing. On top of the usual kind of police infiltrators who will be trooping around the Northwest trying to sell us machine guns, every community must be on the lookout for new "comrades" who just don't seem to be able to behave themselves in public, who are constantly wanting to "do something" which makes us look bad in the eyes of the locals, and who dress in strange and outré garb.

One of my favorite ways to weed out these types is the restaurant test. Take a new "comrade" out to dinner in some reasonably upscale place, say a Golden Corral (that's my idea of upscale), and see if they can sit at a table, have a meal, and conduct a conversation in a normal tone of voice without wearing White Power t-shirts, shouting foul language and racial epithets, or throwing cream pies at the customers.

Just Say No to GUBU

So how do we fight off the Hidden Hand in the Homeland?

The solution to this problem is the same as the solution to virtually all of our others. We just say no. We grow up and comport ourselves like adults, and we do not tolerate those whose agenda, for whatever reason, clearly involves the deliberate disruption of what we are trying to do. We are constantly accused by our enemies of being intolerant; the sorry fact is that we are entirely too tolerant of entirely too much by way of bizarre and dysfunctional behavior on the part of pretty much anyone who claims to be "one of us". The enemy knows this and has taken advantage of this trait of ours for generations. Tolerance of what is wrong is complicity in what is wrong, and that applies to our wee Movement as much as to anything else.

It's so simple. We say no to GUBU. We say no to childish nonsense and we do not allow among us those who say yes. If you were being paid to build someone a house, would you tolerate a mentally retarded and delusional carpenter who went around smashing the fixtures with a sledge hammer? There is an old joke about a village idiot who ran into a doctor's office. He then began to jump up and down on one foot while waving his arms like windmills and snapping his head back and forth. "Doc, Doc, you got to help me !" the idiot cried. "It hurts when I do this!"

"Well then, don't *do* that!" said the exasperated doctor.

We are not idiots, at least we aren't if we will exert the most rudimentary effort of will necessary to stop waving our arms and snapping our heads back and forth as if we were in the grip of some kind of political St. Vitus's dance. There is no reason on earth why we cannot come to a mutual agreement that we are simply going do stop doing it. It's not hard. The Hidden Hand is there and it will continue to be there, but we have sure given it a hell of a lot to work with. Because dead serious, guys—we really haven't got a whole lot of time left.

We Face the First Test

My Racial Comrades and Brothers:

This is one that I had hoped against hope I would never have to write, but no such luck, it appears. I have been reluctant to face this issue head on because of all the largely spurious accusations against me down through the years that I "spread division". It's made me a bit gun-shy when a genuinely divisive issue arises, but things have reached the point where this particular topic has to be addressed, frontally and four-square.

I won't beat around the bush. The issue is simple. I need for all of you to decide, in the privacy of your own thoughts, whether your involvement in "this thing of ours" is based on love and fear for the continued existence of our own people, or blind and unthinking hatred for members of other races.

A little over two years ago, the NSNet list got into a somewhat similar situation, although it was by no means as serious as this. I refer to our little teapot tempest at the time of the Elian Gonzalez episode. I ventured to suggest that when armed SWAT teams break into a private home and kidnap a child on the orders of the highest Federal law enforcement officer in the land, that child's race is irrelevant, and that this is a sinister development regarding the ongoing Federal abuse of power which concerns us all.

My God! You would have thought I'd pissed in the punchbowl! There are still some who to this day denounce me as a Jew (??) and a spic-lover because I dared to suggest that maybe children being dragged out of their homes by Federal gangsters with machine guns was something we ought to be concerned about. The present situation is far more serious than the fate of one little Cuban mestizo. We are now entering a period of history when it is entirely possible that the fate of our people may be decided for us, before we have had a chance to seize control of our destiny through the creation of our own nation-state in the Pacific Northwest. It is absolutely essential that our minds be clear on what is happening here, and that we adopt a policy toward these events designed to secure the existence of our people and a future for White children.

Now, before I proceed, one demurrer. This C-Gram is largely directed at Americans. I understand that our European comrades have a much different slant on this and I understand how they can legitimately hold some of the opposing views they do. More on that later on.

A Government of Fruit Loops

In a few months, perhaps even in a few weeks, for the first time in our history, the United States of America will launch a completely unprovoked war of invasion and conquest against another country. Unless some kind of Tonkin incident is in the making, this time there will not even be so much as a legal fig-leaf for this naked, unadorned act of pure brigandage. The impending American invasion of Iraq has nothing whatsoever to do with the events of 9/11, or with Saddam Hussein's mythical "weapons of mass destruction". I have heard all of Bush and Cheney's natter on the alleged reasons for the coming war, and they are all purest bullshit. The true purpose of this war of conquest is threefold:

A) To seize control of the Basra oil fields for the personal benefit of the Bush family and their cronies in the big oil industry, and to set the stage for a second war of conquest to seize the oil fields of Saudi Arabia.

B) To begin the process of destroying all of Israel's enemies in the Middle East, and to give the butcher Ariel Sharon an excuse to "transfer", i.e. drive three million Palestinians out of their homes on the West Bank and Gaza and into Jordan and Egypt as refugees, thus setting the stage for Greater Israel. (Many people do not know that the two blue bars on the Israeli flag, above and below the Star of David, stand for "between the rivers"...the Nile and the Euphrates, the lands that the Jews demand for Greater Israel.)

C. To humiliate and degrade the religion of Islam in the name of looney-tune Christian fundamentalism. Son of Big Iraq Attack is, indeed,

158

part of the Ninth Crusade.

The above state of affairs is made possible by a truly unholy alliance in our government between big oil, Zionism, and wigged-out Christian fundamentalism. I should confess by way of mea culpa that in November of 2000 I supported Bush in the face of the Democrats' blatant attempt to steal the presidential election through jiggery-pokery in Florida. I thought Bush was a simpleton and a dufus, controlled by big business, but at least he *had* to be better than another for years of Clintonism. Hoo boy, little did I know!

I believe it was Sam Francis who coined the term the War Party for this evil coalition of special interests, and it is a good one. The government of the United States has now been completely hijacked by this coalition of big oil interests (Cheney and the Enron crew), neo-conservative Jews who are pulling the strings from behind the scenes (Richard Perle, Ari Fleischer, Paul Wolfowitz, Irving Kristol et. al.), Jewish messianic nutballs in Israel like Sharon and Effi Eitam and the holy Rabbi Ovadia who announced a while back that his excrement was sacred, and finally fruit-loop Christian fundamentalists of the Late Great Planet Earth school like John Ashcroft, Bush himself, Pat Robertson, etc.

Frankly, those tub-thumping Bible-punching Judeo-Christian fools with nothing but pork fat between their ears like Ashcroft and Robertson scare me more than the others combined. I grew up around these people, my first wife was ensnared by them, and I can assure you, they genuinely *believe* that shit. They genuinely believe it to be their religious duty to start a holocaust in the Middle East so that everbuddy kin git *raptured* and JEEEZUS gone come and split the sky open and 144,000 righteous Jews in Izrul is gone suddenly accept JEEEZUS as thar personal savior and go runnin' down into a hole while the anti-Christ (Saddam) blows up the world with nuclear weapons....Guys, no joke. I remember the first Big Iraq Attack; I was working in North Carolina at the time at a major technology company, and I heard men and women whom I had previously considered to be sane screaming their demand that Bush One launch nuclear weapons and murder untold millions of people in order to fulfill Biblical prophecy.

Explain to me, exactly, why it is we should not be concerned about people like that with their finger on the red button? (Sigh) Never mind.

Okay, moving right along here....

There is another thing I remember from that time, and it is more to the point of this C-Gram. I saw a TV news clip of some good ole boys marching down the street in Louisburg, NC, baseball caps on and beer bellies all a -jiggle, carrying signs that said "Bomb Iran Back Into The Stone Age."

Just one problem. We were about to attack Iraq, not Iran. The fact that up until a year before Saddam's Iraq had been our valiant ally against the dreaded Persians was so far over their heads that I never even bothered to try and explain it to any of them. ("Oceania is at war with Eurasia...Oceania has *always* been at war with Eurasia.") These idiots not only didn't know the difference between Iran and Iraq, they didn't even care. They didn't know a Jew from a Juicemaster. They had no idea that the real reason behind Big Iraq Attack was that Bush One was afraid his family's oil properties in Bahrain would be threatened, and that cutting Iraqi oil off the market would drive up the price and put many more millions into the Bush family's pockets. All those numb-nuts could think about was bomb, bomb, bomb, kill, kill, kill the wogs. Yes! Here at long last was some kind of socially acceptable violence against people with dark skins that they could engage in (vicariously, of course), laugh at, holler over, crow about, without running into the wall of political correctness that forbids White males from uttering even the most tentative, timorous peep against any protected, dark minority. All of a sudden there was one dark-skinned minority that was no longer protected, against whom years of (thoroughly justified) rage and hate and bitterness at the loss of our country to mud people could safely and openly be vented. They didn't care why; all of a sudden they knew that they could lash out against certain people with dark skins not only safely, but with a measure of the social and peer approval that the White male craves above all else.

The lesson was not lost on Bush Two. It is said that every society has to have a scapegoat. In view of the rising unemployment, the crumbling stock market, the collapsing infrastructure, corporate corruption scandals, and increasing social dysfunction, all of a sudden we have the War On Terror and a dark-skinned minority who can now be safely vented against, all our frustrations channeled against...while the Jew remains in the background, behind the curtain, pulling the strings and manipulating the smoke and the mirrors. Okay, this is already running long and we still have quite a way to go, so I will avoid the temptation to go off into a long dissertation here and try to drag myself back to the point.

Son of Big Iraq Attack

As you may have noticed, I oppose the war on Iraq and I have forwarded a number of articles to the list, some of them by leftists, some of them even by Jews like Uri Avnery, in an effort to try and give my readers some kind of perspective on what is going on here and why it is important. A living example of politics making strange bedfellows, I agree, but I suspect we're going to be seeing quite a lot of that. For example, I personally believe we need to be getting involved in the anti-globalization movement, but let's don't even go there, yet.

Over the past few weeks I have been getting a small but somewhat increasing number of responses from people along the lines of am I some kind of Arab-lover? Am I doing a Povl Riis-Knudsen and screwing a Palestinian woman? (No) Am I insane? (Probably, to devote my entire life to this mess) and finally kill kill kill wogs wogs wogs kill wogs kill wogs aaaarrrrrggh gaaaaaaccck kill kill tee hee hee gglllll

Okay, let's start with the basics. Let's assume my entire career for the past 30 years never happened. Here is a basic statement of my own beliefs on this subject.

*Do I believe Arabs to be our racial equals? No.

*Do I believe Arabs should be in this country running all the Subways and feeling up the White high school girls they hire for counter help? No.

*Do I believe Arabs should be knocking up dumb-ass White bimbos, marrying them to get green cards, and then running off with the half-breed kids to Jordan or Egypt? No on the knocking up and the marriage because they shouldn't be here at all, yes on the running away to the Middle East with the half-breeds once the foul deed is done. I might add

161

that in most of these cases, the Arab fathers have stated to Islamic courts that their reason for fleeing America with their children was because they didn't want their sons to grow up as bird-brained Beavises with their caps on backwards good for nothing except playing computer games, and their daughters to grow up to be drug-addicted sluts, for which I don't blame them one damned bit.

*Do I believe that Arabs should be here at all? No.

*Do I believe that we have the right to invade Arab countries, brutalize and humiliate them, and steal their oil to line the pockets of Texas oil moguls and to remove any threat to the bandit state of Israel? No, I do not.

*Do I believe that we owe the Palestinian people respect and moral support in their heroic battle against Israel? Yes.

*Do I believe that a man like the father of four who recently strapped an explosive belt around his waist, went into Tel Aviv and gave up his own life so that his children might one day be free to live as Muslims in their own land, is a better man than the so-called Aryan Warrior who talks big and brave on his computer and then screams for me to remove him from the list when I accidentally hit "CC" instead of "BCC" and reveal his email address? Yes, as a matter of fact, I do.

*Do I believe that as a mark of respect for the unimaginable suffering that this small nation of dark-skinned people is undergoing at the hands of the enemies of all mankind, we should at least do them the courtesy of refraining from calling them "sand niggers" and other racial slurs? Yes, I do.

*In view of the fact that every bullet, every bomb, every electric cattle prod, every bulldozer and every Jewish settlement is paid for with American tax dollars, do I believe that the Arabs are entirely justified in viewing America as an enemy? Yes, I do.

* Should we be concerned about the possible domino effect that the presently impending attack on Iraq might trigger, including possible Arab retaliation in this country that might kill many White people? In the name of all sanity, yes!

*Do I believe that there are many unanswered questions about exactly what happened on September 11th, 2001 and that we need to treat that as a case of the jury still being out rather than swallowing our government's official version wholesale? Yes, I do. *Is it possible that 9/11 was a black

162

op designed to give the War Party an excuse to launch a campaign of world conquest and oil seizure? I find that to be a distinct possibility.

*In other words, could we be bombing and killing completely innocent people for no reason other than to protect Israel and steal the oil? Oh, yes.

In 25 words or less: they have no right to be here and we have no right to be there. Neither do we have the right to bomb them, murder them, invade their countries, insult their religion and steal their oil.

There you have it.

Now, About You...

Now, what you are going to have to decide is whether you can live with these opinions of mine. They won't change, I assure you. I really wish that this was a minor, one-shot deal like the Elian Gonzalez thing. Unfortunately, this whole issue is something that we are going to have to be dealing with for many years. Mr. Bush evidently intends to see to that.

I understand a few things. First off, I have noticed down through the years that every White racialist has his own personal racial bugaboos (or jigaboos). Especially in the South, we get old Klan types for whom it will always be niggerniggernigger and all this Jew stuff is just a distraction by "Natzies". For Californians and Texans, the worst scourge will always be Mexicans. In Canada it's Indians and Pakis. I knew a Swede once who literally frothed at the mouth at the mention of gypsies. With me, it used to be niggers when I was in high school. Then I joined the NSWPP and did the duty desk on Franklin Road, and I took those hate calls from those New York Jews and heard pure evil coming out of that receiver. From that point on, for me it has always been the kike that makes my skin crawl, on a personal level.

But for some—especially in Europe—it's Arabs. I understand this, especially in our comrades from European countries who are surrounded by them due to the unlimited immigration from Morocco and Algeria and Turkey, etc. Again I say, I can understand why a European cannot quite grok what I am saying, and I repeat that I am speaking here as an

163

American, to Americans. This is as it should be, because America is the problem. We're the ones who are about to start this insane war of conquest that may impact on the whole world in generations to come. But there are some Americans, as I am learning, to whom an Arab is simply the ultimate in Third World horror. The very thought of an Arab causes these people to fall down in a frothing, raving, grand mal epileptic seizure. I know because I have gotten the e-mail equivalents of said grand mal.

Guys, you know what I am trying to do here. I am desperately, frantically, in agony trying to get you people to come to this unspeakably beautiful land and make it a home for all our people. I am not concerned with killing anyone, except insofar as that will eventually become necessary for the survival of my own race and civilization. As Clausewitz wrote, war is simply politics by other means. But we cannot ignore what is going on in the wider world, and what is about to happen will have serious effects on our whole movement (the Northwest movement, which is the only one we have any more and the only one worth worrying about.)

Realpolitik

The Germans, as always, have a word for the course that we must adopt, with relation to the Iraq war and everything else. It is called *realpolitik,* i.e. a politics based in the real world, not the virtual world of cyberspace or the dream world of pure ideology unencumbered by practical considerations.

What are the *realpolitik* principles we must follow in the establishment of the Northwest Republic?

1. We must all *Come Home* and Come Home *now* while it is still possible to do so legally and there is still an essentially sound economy here, with jobs available. We have to get our first wave of settlers on the way *now.*

2. Our independence will not come about until the central government in Washington DC is sufficiently weak so that it can no longer respond to political and paramilitary insurrection with overwhelming force. (Thanks to Thomas the Rhymer for the wording on that one.)

3. The coming war of conquest in the Middle East will accelerate that degenerative process...eventually. Here is where we run up against a bit of a problem. I have had some e-mails and letters from people who say that we need to be *encouraging* the coming war so as to speed up the Federal government's decline, even to the point of allying ourselves with right-wing Jews. (Yes, one guy actually said that.) Well, at least some people are thinking, up to a point, and saying something besides killwogs, killwogs, killwogs, so kudos to them for it.

First of all, we do not ally ourselves with Jews. Not *ever.* That is the one absolute red line we simply *do not* cross. Because if we do, then what the hell is the point of any of it?

Secondly, the war *is* coming. Whether or not I, or any of us, oppose it is actually moot. White people are completely powerless, and our opposition or approval will make no difference one way or the other. What are we going to do to stop it? Send one another newspaper clippings and e-mails? Realpolitik aside, at the moment, taking the moral high ground against world conquest by ZOG is a luxury we can afford.

Thirdly, while launching a war of conquest in the Middle East will eventually cause the ZOG regime to overextend itself and become too weak to hold onto everything, we need to worry about the short-term effects on ourselves, including increased government surveillance and police powers, increased detention without trial, the institution of some kind of civilian version of the secret military tribunals for "domestic terrorism", and above all the possible restriction of movement within the United States, either through total economic collapse or through the promulgation of a Soviet-style work permit and internal passport system. There have already been a few trial balloons sent up on this in the form of proposals for a national ID card. In theory, a long and costly foreign war is always good for revolutionaries, yes...but not now. We are simply too unprepared. If only we hadn't wasted all those years...God *damn* the Nude Emperors! ! Sorry, where was I?

4. The creation of a new nation-state must be an act of realpolitik, i.e. it must be done on a real-world basis and real-world strategies and tactics have to apply. And in the real world, that may well mean that here in the Northwest, we may end up with more than a few of those strange bedfellows that real politics makes.

Including, possibly, Arabs at some point in the future.

I really hesitated to mention this, because I can hear it now...."Harold is just sucking up to Arabs in the hopes that they will give him money, blah, blah, blah." But while honesty may not always be the best policy, it is always mine. So, guys, let's state the obvious here. There may come a time when it is in the interests of the Islamic world to open a "second front" here in North America, and when that time comes, it would be a good idea if we don't have a paper trail or cyber-trail of calling them sand niggers and ragheads. In today's present atmosphere it's probably better that I don't pursue this line of exposition any further, since I am sure this list is monitored, but let me put it this way:

I would never be dumb enough to do a Pierce and let somebody hand me $300,000 in a briefcase that I knew damned well came from an armored car robbery. But....let's say some Mohammed or Achmed were to pitch up and offer financing for a proper Northwest independence movement, and I could be convinced it was on the level, wasn't an FBI sting, and that I could legally accept the funds. (And I would take a *hell* of a lot of convincing, I promise you.) Would I take it? For the sake of securing the existence of my people and a future for white children? You bet your bippy. Nor is this unprecedented. Remember the trips some of our people like James Warner and Don Andrews took to Libya in the late 1980s?

There is a story told about the Roman emperor Vespasian. The imperial treasury was broke, but rather than impose a new tax Vespasian actually opened the world's first chain of public pay toilets all around Rome. His son Titus, who later became emperor himself, protested that this was a dirty way to raise funds. Vespasian tossed him a nice shiny silver denarius coin. "Is this not good silver?" he asked his son.

"Yes," replied Titus.

"That's odd, since it was crap this morning," replied the emperor.

So, is this one of my practical reasons for giving the Arabs at least moral support in their struggle against the Zionists in Tel Aviv and Washington? Yes, and I make no apology for it. Will it ever actually happen? Probably not, but why burn that particular bridge even if we may never come to it? *Realpolitik,* people, real politics.

166

Yes, It Really Is The Jews, Stupid!

Finally, there is another aspect of this that I want to deal with. Again I apologize for the length of this piece, but it's necessary.

A few days ago I sent out a superb monograph by Edgar Steele called "It's The Jews, Stupid!" I assume most of you got it; if not, let me know and I'll resend it. This C-Gram will in future be my canned answer to questions on the Arab sitch, but when I send this in the future I will accompany it with "It's The Jews, Stupid!" Because that says it all.

If there is one thing that is blindingly clear to everyone, it is that the Jews *want* this war. They are about to be overrun demographically as the Palestinians outbreed them almost three to one, and it is essential that they have American cover for their policy of "transfer", i. e. mass deportation of the Palestinians from their land.

The survival of our race and our civilization depends on two things and two things only. These are:

1. A complete change in ourselves, including a fearless confrontation with the issue of *character* and a spiritual transformation within the collective soul of our racially aware community, and

2. A thoroughly internalized awareness of the overriding primacy of the Jewish question as it affects our continued existence.

No other issue of race, culture, religion, politics or economics is so vitally central to our continued existence as a people as the Jewish question. The Jew is an infection in the body of humanity and the root cause of every disease we have, including the character issue, because what has made us weak and lazy and cowardly is our adoption of the Jewish world view of pure materialism. It is not just our moral obligation to oppose the Jew in every aspect of life, it is an urgent requirement for our survival. Over the past century we have failed to understand this overriding reality and failed to act upon it, and we now see the result of that failure all around us.

We must oppose this war for all the very reasons that the Jew so urgently desires it. We must hasten the exit from the world stage of the bandit state of Israel, through the Palestinian bomb and the Palestinian birthrate. We must do everything possible to undermine and subvert the current regime of the War Party, because in it we see the both the neo-conservative racial Jews and the tub-thumping fundamentalist spiritual Jews displaying their naked power and their lust for blood and conquest and messianic madness. It is inevitable that their madness, sooner or later, will make White people bleed. The late Robert Miles once called Judaism a state of mind, the best definition I have ever heard, and it is this state of mind we must battle against with every weapon at our command.

In the final analysis, we must oppose this war because *it is the right thing to do,* because we cannot allow the Jew to exercise this kind of world-destroying power. If that means that as a matter of tactics, not ideology, we have to lay off the sand-nigger spiel for a while, then that much at least we can do. Remember, at least at first, it is their people who will be doing the dying under the terrible Judeo-American bombs. We may not love these people, but we can at least have the decency to look on at their heartbreaking sacrifice with the respect of silence. And when they do strike back at the murderers of their children, as any race of people will do however ineffectually, we can refrain from losing our sense of proportion and always remember why...and remember the fact that we started it all when we so spinelessly handed our government and our country over to the kike.

What Now?

Okay, I'll wind this up.

First off, the intention of this C-Gram is to explain my position on this issue once and for all. I have done that, at regrettable length. It is not my purpose to begin a long, pissing-contest debate over this issue. We debate too much and act too little anyway.

Accordingly, I will publish no responses to this C-Gram in the NS Forum on either side. The Forum will concentrate on what is important, the creation of a new homeland for our people. If you want to discuss the Arab thing further, e-mail me and I will speak to you privately about it. But you do have to make a decision, and that is in regards to your own further participation in the Northwest idea. You must understand that this is going to be a real-world event and that if you continue to be involved you will have to come to terms with *realpolitik,* on this issue and no doubt a host of others. That is something we've never been very good at. We far prefer arguing about how many Stormtroopers can dance on the head of a pin to the deadly serious business of revolution and nation-building.

If my attitude towards Muslims and my insistence on opposing a United States government which has gone insane really, honest to God bothers you to the point where you simply can't get around it, then feel free to unsubscribe. I don't want to waste your time, and I don't want you wasting mine.

If you're ready to get real and get on with it, stick around. I promise you, it will be one hell of a ride.

The Street-Walking Rationale

[Caveat: This article refers to the situation in North America, not in Europe, where different conditions and strategic situations apply. - HAC]

One of the Racially Conscious Community's most durable and sacrosanct sacred cows is the street-walk, otherwise known, almost always incorrectly, as a rally. (18 people do not constitute a rally of any kind, although the leftist counter-demonstrations are often sufficiently large to merit that designation.)We recently had an example of this in Gainesville, Florida. Since my duty station within the Racially Conscious Community is to ask questions regarding sacred cows that no one wants to answer, and to discuss things in public that the self-appointed leadership do not want discussed, I reckon it's about time I pointed out the nudity of this particular emperor again. Quite a few of us seem to be politely and deferentially averting our eyes from the fact that he's butt-nekkid. This exposition on the said sacred cow will inevitably be construed as an "attack" on Billy Roper. It is nothing of the kind, of course, but under RCC protocol any public discussion of a problem or issue that the self-appointed leadership does not wish discussed is dismissed as an "attack", thus alleviating any necessity that they answer any uncomfortable questions or justify themselves and their assorted behaviors. This is standard procedure and I don't expect anything different.

To begin with, let me explain the official rationale behind street-walking, point by point. Street-walking in theory is essentially an attempt to reproduce here in America certain specific objective conditions which apply to Europe today, or which have applied to Europe in the past, or which to a limited extent applied to America in a largely idealized and incorrectly perceived past, viz. the 50,000-man Klan marches of the 1920s, etc. More specifically, street-walking is an attempt to replicate here, in the 21st century, certain key periods in European history which provided windows of opportunity for revolution, specifically Weimar Germany and to a lesser extent Petrograd in 1917 for leftists. (They have this same obsession as well.) It's a form of what anthropologists call sympathetic magic. The belief is that if we emulate the behavior of certain political movements from these historical epochs, and put on an approximate pastiche of the costume of the period, then somehow the year 2003 will *become* these historical epochs. Or maybe 2004 or 2010 or 2020.

Here's how it's supposed to work, in theory:

1. We begin with a small number of people, mostly socially dysfunctional young men plus a few older right-wing cranks. (Guys, I'm sorry, but those of you who have actually attended these gigs will recognize the truth of what I say. There is no longer anything to be gained, and much to be lost, by glossing over uncomfortable truth.) This small handful of people then goes out in public, often oddly dressed and waving signs and flags from the various historical epochs they are trying to invoke. Under the protection of the government's police, they exchange shouts and shoves and largely harmless missiles with various Reds, mud people, bugger boys, etc. So far, so good.

2. This street theater generates Establishment media publicity, which according to orthodox Movement thinking is the be-all, end-all, and absolute lifeblood of our struggle. According to this school of thought, to be on TV is to be real, the goods, the real stuff, the right stuff. True, we can usually get a few sound bytes on the six and eleven o'clock news with these activities, and sometimes a couple of hourly mentions on CNN and a few mangled newspaper quotes as well.

3. In theory, other White people will see this publicity, admire the hell out of us, and come clamoring to join our grouplets and go on the next such activity. Here's where the whole concept starts to wobble and slip, but let's leave that for later.

4. With every new street-walk, there will (in theory) be more and more White people wearing the costumes, waving the signs and flags, and screaming and shouting at the Reds and muds and bugger boys. Eventually there will be thousands of us and we will outnumber the scum. Up to this point, all of this is *theoretically* possible, and on a handful of occasions such as Gage Park and Marquette Park in Chicago, Glenn Miller's White

171

Patriot Party, etc. we have even gotten to within faintly audible shouting distance of this point on the horizon.

5. On those few occasions when we have reached that point, the whole project has always fallen apart due to one of two causes: A) The issue of character, which we as a community steadfastly refuse to confront. (Glenn Miller is a good example here.) Then there's B) The complete and total lack of anything remotely resembling a *plan* to transmute large gatherings of racially aware Whites into a political force that will transfer state power from the hands of those who presently hold it into our own. But usually the process has broken down long before, at Step 3. The necessary connection is not made in the minds of the White masses; the necessary desire to emulate and to join the street-walkers never makes its appearance.

Why not? There are two reasons for this.

First off, there is the fact that the ZOG media controls what, if anything, the White population is allowed to see and hear of such activities. Like all serious stories nowadays from the monkoid sniper in Maryland to the coming invasion of Iraq, our activities are presented not as news, but as *entertainment,* which is what the masses (or Them Asses as an old Wobbly called them) expect from television. "Look at the funny racists in the funny clothes! Now stay tuned for That Seventies Show!"

Does this mean that we would get any better results if all the street-walkers wore suits and ties? No. Because secondly, there is again that issue of White *character* which we refuse to address. This particular uncomfortable manifestation of it is the fact that the overwhelming majority of White people are simply morally incapable of giving us the kind of reaction we want from them. We are speaking to their grandfathers, not to them. Modern-day Boobus Americanus is a moral void. It is useless to appeal to the nobler natures and better instincts of the White majority. They have none, and have been deliberately made that way. They will *never* respond to any kind of mass movement tactics because the necessary moral instincts, frames of reference, and cultural motivations have been socially engineered out of them. We are beating a dead horse.

The Twisting of Rockwell's Legacy

Okay, that's street-walking in theory. But what are we *really* doing here? *Attendez-vous,* guys. Let us start with a little history lesson.

Street-walking in its present racial form in America (Europe is a completely different kettle of fish) goes back to the deservedly famous Commander George Lincoln Rockwell and his early Stormtrooper activities in Washington, D. C. and elsewhere. Since Rockwell was so far head and shoulders above everyone else that the RCC has subsequently produced by way of leadership, self-appointed or otherwise, it is understandable that a lot of misconception and distortion has attached itself to the Rockwell legend. One of the more unfortunate beliefs that has embedded itself in our RCC subculture from the Rockwell era is the concept of the minuscule activity on public property, especially dressed in some kind of odd garb or costume, as a kind of defining rite of passage or manhood ritual. This is a completely incorrect reading of George Lincoln Rockwell's tactics, which just as much as Weimar were distinct and particular to his time and place, a time and place now almost half a century distant. A temporary set of tactics which Rockwell himself defined, repeatedly and very clearly, as *publicity stunts* to be used only during the earliest phases of the ANP's struggle, has become a kind of cult among racially aware Whites.

The core of this belief system is that rather than actually fighting and killing our enemies, as was the case throughout thousands of years of Aryan history, "real White men" now display their macho and their physical prowess by *symbolic gesture,* in a kind of mock ritual combat. The ritual often includes dressing up in strange, historically apocryphal clothing such as home-made costumes patterned after the SA uniforms of the Third Reich, historically inaccurate Ku Klux Klan robes of purple and bilious green, and more recently shaven heads with body tattoos. (Andrew Greenbaum's "uniformed branch" resembled the Village People.) On the street there is much bellicose chanting, shouting, threats, slogans, like gorillas beating their chests; the hurling of rocks and bottles which can be painful but so far never lethal; the mock half-charges and aggressive posturing, etc. In some respects it is remarkably similar to the ritualistic but almost completely non-fatal wars between tribes of New

173

Guinea headhunters, and it seems to serve a similar purpose, including the bonding feast afterwards wherein the enemy (who seem to be in on the play in their own minds, although they'd never admit it) are held to scorn and boasts of great deeds done on the field of battle are proclaimed, etc.

The participants in such activities have come through an event which generated an adrenalin and pheromone rush similar to that produced by actual battle, but with none of the risks. They can subsequently feel the sense of accomplishment and increased self-esteem that comes from the illusory idea that they have fought back, that they are in the trenches and front line soldiers...but no one is actually hurt, not a single weapon is fired, no physical damage of any kind is inflicted on the enemy. On Monday morning they all trudge back to their shitwork jobs, and all is as it was. Everybody is happy.

On a few occasions actual combat does break out, more by accident than anything else, but it is always of short duration and quickly broken up by the police, often with legal consequences which far outweigh any advantage to be gained. (Greensboro and the Palmer House in Chicago, 1977 being a good example.) Before somebody starts yelling about November Third, it needs to be very clearly understood that Greensboro was an accidental exception, totally *sui generis,* and we should note that it has not been allowed to happen again. Thank God. No one but an idiot would want to go through the years that followed Greensboro as the lives of sixteen innocent men were utterly destroyed by this society's obscene judicial process.

The actual chance of anyone getting seriously hurt on one of these street walks, beyond a few bruises, is slim. The police are always out in force and usually more or less do their jobs and prevent the tiny handful of Whites from being lynched by the lefty muddy mobs. There have been some nasty incidents at some of these events when they have been allowed to get out of hand or when the police are absent through design or incompetence, but even when that happens there is never any serious threat to the power structure. If there were, the police would be breaking up such gatherings with rubber bullets and nightsticks, not guarding us.

In essence, street-walks are a psychological substitute for actual physical resistance against the tyranny that is destroying our race. It's rather like the WWF, ritualized mock combat which allows a certain level

174

of self-esteem in those who participate in them, as if exchanging insults and maybe even a few shoves and pokes with scum is in some way equivalent to actual, serious resistance which threatens the power structure. (An interesting digression: while Sinn Fein does hold demonstrations regularly in Ireland, they have the many thousands in numbers needed to do it right, and the actual Volunteers of the I. R.A. are under orders to stay away from such events to prevent their being photographed or arrested. The only exceptions are firing parties at Republican funerals, although I understand the Provos stopped doing that because it was too risky.)

In some ways this cult of false macho is perfectly understandable, in view of the extreme rarity of physical courage among White males these days. I do not deny a certain very limited value in these events; in the absence of a better rite of passage for young White men, this one will have to do for the time being, although I frankly think a better one would be learning a trade and raising a family in the Homeland. But I must admit I like my little aphorism: **"A White man of twenty who doesn't street-walk has no balls. A White man of forty who's still street-walking has no brains."**

Nobody Shows

Rather than run this e-mail to Tolstoyan length trying to prove what should be obvious, I can only point to the one outstanding feature of street-walking that overrides all others: it doesn't work. We've been doing it for almost fifty years now. *It doesn't work.* Barring a major situational change in America (always possible), it ain't never gonna work.

Why doesn't it work? Ask Billy Roper, who planned his event in Gainesville for weeks and then got there to find seventeen people besides himself. (Okay, twenty-three counting the four in the truck who were turned away and the two Christians who refused to participate with people who insulted their faith.) It doesn't work because *nobody shows.*

Why does nobody show? Well, that gets into that character issue we all do double-backed flips to avoid talking about. But ask anyone who has ever tried to organize one of these things. Ask him about the sinking feeling of horror he gets in his gut when the signs are all painted, the flags on the flagpoles, and he looks around and sees them stacked up while in front of him stand ten or twelve or eighteen people who are looking around them and muttering that one question that precedes every such event:

"WHERE THE HELL *IS* EVERYBODY?"

Oh, the ingeniousness of the excuses! I have heard everything from stirring accounts of battles with niggers in convenience stores along the way (that never happened) to "My dog died." Sudden and mysterious car trouble is always a favorite, but above all, there's that hardy perennial "At the last minute I had to work!" Of course, some of them always do manage to make it to the barbecue or potluck afterward, especially if there's free beer in the offing. (You know, that might be a good Forum topic. You guys who have done the sidewalk sashays before, what are some of your favorite excuses you've heard for not showing up? Especially the ones who do manage to appear in time for the feed?)

"But...But...But...."

I understand that I am now going to be pelted with dozens, possibly hundreds, of e-mails from people screaming "Marquette Park!", "Forsyth County", and "Glenn Miller!" at me. [Sigh] Yes. Given a small core of highly active people and above all given something approaching adequate *funding,* it is possible under certain extremely rare and specific conditions to get comparatively significant numbers of White people into the streets for very short periods of time before the social disapproval mechanisms kick in and they go shuffling back into their dens and plop back down in front of the television. It is rare, but it has occurred. It has occurred so rarely that these exceptions prove the rule.

In Marquette and Forsyth there was an immediate, visible threat of nigger invasion. Glenn Miller was one of the beneficiaries of the Order's largess and he had a couple of hundred thou for full-time organizers, actual uniforms as opposed to costumes, paid transport to and from events, etc. If some rich man cares to lay two hundred grand on Billy Roper I'm sure we'll see some vast improvements in his performance as well.

OK, it's now 2003. Where are the results of all of those past "close, but no cigars?" Where are the visible results of any of it for the past 50 years? How much actual political, racial, or demographic *change* has come about, from *any* of it?

Again I ask, point blank: "Is this what we need to be spending the next 30 years doing?" Again I say...it is time for us to sit down, re-assess, and *re-think* all of this.

Building a New White Literature

I wrote my first short story when I was eleven years old. I was rejected by my first Jewish editor when I was twelve.

The short story was a very bad H. P. Lovecraft knock-off. Okay, I have to admit that there are few things more ridiculous than an eleven year-old trying to write like a 19th century Victorian. (Yes, I know Lovecraft wrote during the 1920s and 1930s, but his style was of an earlier epoch.) The Jew in question was one Mrs. Feldman who was faculty adviser to the junior high school newspaper. She said that my story was too long to publish in a stapled sheet periodical mimeographed on construction paper (well, fair enough, it was) but she also accused me of being "pretentious." Why? Why did she feel it necessary to add a gratuitous insult? Unless it was the instinctive Judaic reaction to anything that upholds older Aryan values or culture, an Aryan past, even an outdated literary style? You might say she was the first Goat Dancer.

Why, she asked, didn't I write about something contemporary, like that wonderful Dr. Martin Luther King and his struggle to free the beautiful noble colored people from their bondage to us horrible Southern honkies? I was "wasting my talent" trying to reach outside the parameters of the world as defined by the Jews and their lefty-lib allies. Mustn't waste my talent doing things Yehudi doesn't approve of, eh what?

In 1965 there were probably less than 100 Jews in Burlington, North Carolina, but this woman zeroed in on the one area in her workspace where she could control the flow of creativity and communication among the children and force it to pass a political and social litmus test. I don't think it was some big kosher conspiracy to deny publication to my childish Lovecraft pastiche. I think she did it by simple Hebraic instinct. It's just what Jews *do,* like baby alligators seek water when they hatch. I know that now, but at the time I was baffled and enraged. I have often

178

wondered what would have happened with my life had I received any encouragement at all with my writing and been had I been allowed to write what I *wanted* to write, not confronted with constant demands that I channel my talents into "contemporary" politically and liberally acceptable directions.

There were other incidents of this kind during my junior high and high school years. Even in a Southern mill town like Burlington, there was an embryonic left-liberal cultural establishment, largely centered around Elon College and UNC just up Highway 54, although in those days at least, it kept its head down and moved cautiously, careful not to offend the shoutin' Baptist, Chamber of Commerce ruling strata. I think they may have gathered in covens in the dead of night and bowed low before an idol of Frank Porter Graham. All very progressive, don't y'know.

To cite only one other example, when I attended Governor's School of North Carolina in 1970 in drama, I wanted to do actual *drama.* You know, plays. With actual scripts and dialog. Stage management. Build sets. Acting. Learning lines. Rehearsal. All that yukky disciplined stuff that teaches acting as a serious craft. I ran that by my classmates and the instructors, and you would have thought I'd pissed in the punchbowl. Huh? Discipline? Work? Bummer, man! The screaming queen director from New York city and a small clique of Jewish and left-hippie-pothead students wanted to do hippy-dippy stream of consciousness improv crap emoting about, like, far out, man. I-Da-Gadda-Da-Vida. Groovy, man. Guess who won out?

Again, I wonder where I would have gone had I been able to spend that summer doing genuine, disciplined, serious dramatic study and acting training. I can't help at least some suspicion that's another potential life path those goddamned hippie lefty Jew shits ruined for me. Hell, I might be a Hollywood degenerate as big as John Travolta now! I might have been one of the 1,465 actors who did a nude scene with Susan Sarandon, or even one of the 270 who did one on camera. I might have been found floating face down in my swimming pool at age 29, dead from an overdose of freebase. The damned kikes denied me my potential!

Okay, getting back to fiction. I wrote my first novel, *Rose of Honor,* at sixteen and was rejected by my first Jewish literary agent at age seventeen,

179

a hose-nosed hebe I'd picked out of a Writer's Digest ad named A. L. Fierst. Mr. Fierst took my fee of $35 and sent my manuscript back saying he'd only read a few pages of it and he wouldn't handle me because "you have a chip on your shoulder." To this day, I have no idea on earth what the asshole meant by that remark. It didn't seem to me to have anything to do with the novel. Some of you read *Rose of Honor* when I finally got it published 30 years later. Maybe you can tell me. There is only one overtly anti-Jew reference in the entire book and that was a completely accurate historic one about a minor character in the Wars of the Roses in the fifteenth century. I wasn't even an anti-Semite when I wrote the book, I was a teenaged kid with a Byron complex projecting his own mixed-up adolescent experiences onto a historical fictional backdrop, convinced of course that I was doing the most clever and original thing in the world.

I was, however, beginning to notice some things about the publishing industry. I was coming to recognize Jewish names when I saw them, and it seemed to me there sure were a lot of Jewish names in publishing. It started with the literary agents who even then were becoming the first line of kosher defense, the first Hebraic hurdle a budding author had to cross. The days of dog-eared, coffee-stained book manuscripts coming "over the transom" onto an editor's desk and a new John Steinbeck suddenly being discovered thereby ended in the 1950s. Today, not only do editors refuse even to glance at unagented material, but most *agents* won't even take new authors without exorbitant "reading fees" which are simply a scam to rip-off wannabe writers. There are whole agencies like that, notably Scott Meredith, an agency that does represent some major authors, to be sure, but that has acquired an evil reputation down through the years as a racket ripping off new writers for every reading and "revision" fee they can drain from the poor bastards.

The first thing a serious agency that really does market literary properties for publication will want to know is a detailed bio of yourself, with the most important section being "creative references"—teachers, college professors, other writers, people in the publishing industry, people in the media, and the more "steins" and "bergs" in those names the better. In other words, *who do you know?* Who can vouch for your Politically Correct bona fides? In the publishing industry this is known as having a "rabbi", either a real one complete with *shul* and sheeny beanie, or else in the vernacular, a well-placed contact, a patron, someone who can show you the ropes, guide you along, give you advice, get you connected with the right people. Many agents will admit openly to their prospects, "You gotta have a rabbi. No rabbi, we don't touch you. Too many possibilities for surprises later in the day."

Many literary agencies hire private detectives to do full background checks on authors before agreeing to take them on as clients. They explain this by telling us, quite accurately, that to a major publisher nowadays an author is a total package, not just what he writes. It is a brutal and effective screening process that someone like me simply cannot survive. I know because I have tried to get agented and only succeeded once, with a real maverick. I have a paper trail of Political Incorrectness.

The days of Thomas Wolfe's literary agent flying down to Asheville from New York once a week, letting himself into Wolfe's house with his own key, stepping over Wolfe's snoring drunken body passed out on the kitchen floor, gathering up every piece of paper he could find in the house with typewriting on it from the tables, chairs, laundry hamper, etc. (Wolfe wrote standing up, typing on a manual typewriter on top of his refrigerator) and then taking the whole lot back to New York to sort it out into a novel—those days are long gone. Nowadays no eccentric literary geniuses need apply. An author is a literary property just as much as his work, and he must have no embarrassing political, racial, or social skeletons in his closet that might interfere with marketing. It's not quite the same thing, but look at the flak Mel Gibson caught even before *The Passion* when his *father's* Tridentine Catholicism, never mind his own religious views came out in the media.

Then once you do get agented, there's the manuscript readers. Assuming your manuscript gets to a System publishing house at all, it is tossed to a reader before an editor even looks at the title page. The reader is almost certain to be out of Columbia or CUNY. Ninety-five percent of all System publishing is still centered in Jew York City. (Those publishing
imprints and literary agents who have left because of the terrible expense of doing business there or other reasons are excoriated, viz. "they can't make it in the Big Apple so they cut and ran." Most of them don't last

181

except for agencies in California who specialize in movie scripts and screenplays. The kikes are always very big on centralized control and monitoring of any industry or enterprise they run.) Your reader will be Jewish, feminist, queer, or some combination of the three. I mean at least ninety percent of them, some combination of the three. Seriously. This sitch has gotten so notorious in the industry that even some Jewish and leftist male writers are starting to protest about it. If the reader trashes your book, back it goes to the literary agent. An editor never even sees it. Then you run the gauntlet of the editors themselves—Jews, feminists, faggots, lefties, or all of the above. But no individual editor makes a decision to publish any more. There are editorial boards, committees who review and pick over the recommendations of the individual editors. Guess who sits on those boards?

At some stage marketing gets involved to determine if the book has profit potential. You may well be the next Jack Kerouac, but you'd damned well better convince those marketing goblins that you're the next Stephen King, because if they think you won't sell in the millions of bucks, your book gets nowhere near the printing presses. Then there's publishers and publishing house executives themselves. Guess what racial heritage predominates there? To this very day, there is no industry on earth that is more Jew-ridden and under such total Jewish control as Establishment book publishing, with the very similar exception of Hollywood and the movie-making industry.

But that has now changed. Ironically, for all my fulminations against the internet, it is the net which has made it possible to break the iron grip of five or six Jewish-owned multi-national corporations on the book and literary world.

It is called **print-per-order self-publishing.** This is not "vanity publishing" in the old sense. You do pay a small fee for computerized typesetting, depending on the marketing plan you choose. (iUniverse charges $99 for their most affordable plan.) And that's it. The company does do basic marketing for you, listing your books on Amazon.com, with Ingram, Barnes and Noble etc. When someone orders a book on the internet or over the counter at Borders or Waldenbooks, a copy is printed and shipped, either direct to the customer or to the store where the customer can pick it up. I now have eleven novels published; without print-per-order none of them would have ever seen the light of day in my lifetime. I know, because I tried for years to get my fiction published by the Establishment, even to the point of including minor bits of politically correct crap in an effort to "sneak up on the Jews." None of it worked.

When, oh when will we learn? We will *never* be able to "sneak up on the Jews." They are the world's epitomic sneakers. Sneaking is what they do. We will *never* be able to beat them at their own game. Every time that we have defeated the Jews in the past, it is because we have forced them out from behind their protective shields of law and money and made them play *our* people's game, with fire and sword. But I digress.

At one stage I actually had one of the rare remaining gentile, heterosexual male literary agents in California who liked my material and tried to market one of my books, *Bonnie Blue Murder*. It is also one of my more overtly anti-Jewish works, but he so liked the Civil War detective mystery that he agreed to give it a go. (I always suspected he was none too happy about Jewish predominance in his industry.) After a year he came back and reported failure. It wasn't even the Jew thing, according to him. None of the readers or editors he tried even got that far. The problem with *Bonnie Blue* was that no one in Establishment publishing was even willing to consider a novel with a Confederate hero.

Through a good friend in Canada who knows how to build web sites, I published a couple of my novels on the internet in 1999, and got maybe a couple of dozen readers. Then in the year 2000, a comrade to whom I will be eternally grateful sent me an article on print-per-order, and I took it from there. In 2000 and 2001, I had the incredible experience of publishing a lifetime of literary work in a period of about eighteen months.

HAC Is a Hack

Look, let's get something clear here. Charles Dickens I ain't. Ernest Hemingway I ain't. Robert A. Heinlein, not by a long shot. I am a hack. I admit it. Some of my plots and characters are pretty juvenile still, not just because I was juvenile when I wrote them, but because I'd write a book and lug it around the world with me for ten or fifteen years and never really had a chance to sit down and flesh them all out properly.

183

More than once I have tromped through Heathrow or the ferry terminal at Dun Laoghaire or Jan Smuts International in Johannesburg, or elsewhere, staggering out into the early morning of a foreign country with o place to go, lugging a suitcase that weighed about 60 pounds with a dozen typed manuscripts and bits and pieces of manuscripts, a Sears manual typewriter, and a few changes of socks and underwear—all my worldly possessions along with the clothes I had on my back. The last time I had to reduce my life to a single suitcase was in 1998, for an emergency trip to Ireland, but that time I was able to use 3.5" diskettes— ah, technology! But literary hack or not, from now on, if ever I am forced back into single-suitcase mode, I don't have to drag all those manuscripts with me. I may not have sold many copies of my novels, but from now on they are permanently on the record, with the publisher but also on the net and with the Library of Congress and a couple of other places. Pulp fiction as it all may be, at least I know it will now survive me, so that a thousand years from now someone can read *Rose of Honor* or *Slow Coming Dark* or *The Madman and Marina,* if perchance anyone is interested. My literary contributions will be there, and so can yours. So far as I know, the only other racialist to make use of print-per-order is James Michael Butler, who published his novel "One Last Time" about six months ago with iUniverse. Ed Steele was asking me about print-per-order a while back and I am really looking forward to any book he writes, but I don't know what came of it.

I am quite surprised that we don't make any more use of this incredible tool than we do, but then hey, that's our Racially Conscious Community, all right. We never miss an opportunity to miss an opportunity.

There have, of course, been works of racial fiction published prior to the advent of print-per-order. These books were published through private printing, in bulk, and at great expense. Private printers who will print overtly racial works make you pay through the nose. Nor was the technical quality of the books very good. The prototype for them all was Eric Thomson's *The Chosen One,* published in Rhodesia in 1974. There was *The Turner Diaries* of course, followed by *Hunter,* followed by *The Serpent's Walk* and *Hear The Cradle Song* and Tom Chittum's *Civil War I.* Although they weren't strictly speaking fiction, at least not officially, there were also the tens of thousands of copies of the various Klassen books that Alte Benig had privately printed, thus illustrating the limitations of our doing our own printing.

The first thing you need is a deep pocket with mucho bucks. Then there is the problem of storing huge case lots of books somewhere, requiring warehouse or other storage space that usually costs many shekels. Then once all the copies are gone, arranging for a re-print is often a Herculean task. When a racial book goes out of print in the traditional manner, it often stays out of print for fifty years. With print-per-order, that doesn't happen, at least in theory. The industry is still too new for it to have shown how it will stand the test of time, but if it fulfills its promise, then fifty years from now someone will be able to hit some futuristic internet device and order up a copy of *Fire and Rain* or *Hill of the Ravens,* as new and crisply printed as the first copies I pulled out of the shipping case in my respective Texas and Washington cardboard boxes.

I am often asked if print-per-order is practicable for political usage by "our" side. Well, *so far,* yes, it seems they genuinely do adhere to the First Amendment, or more likely they simply don't care what you write so long as your credit card for the typesetting fee is good. Their contracts contain all kinds of disclaimers freeing the publisher from any liability. So far as I am aware, none have been seriously sued or harassed yet over content of their published material. We'll see how they stand up when someone in power notices *Slow Coming Dark* or *The Hill of the Ravens* or something else Politically Incorrect.

The first one I ever submitted for publication to iUniverse was *Slow Coming Dark,* which as those of you who have read it will be aware, says some very unkind things about Billyboy and also about our illustrious present junior Senator from New York. I did it almost as an experiment just to see how they'd react. To my surprise, the publisher didn't bat an eyelash over the anti-Clinton content. What they *were* afraid of was that Alicia Silverstone was going to sue me. They wanted to put in a long legal disclaimer at the beginning which would in my view have marred the book. I was eventually able to talk them down to "The Clintons are real. This book is fiction."

I was holding my breath over *The Hill of the Ravens* all the time it was in editorial, but I never got a peep over the content or my use of the forbidden N word. This genuinely surprised me. In THOR I do something which has been forbidden in Western society since the Middle Ages—I speak of the death of the king, always a treasonable offense, but since 9/11 much more so in this country. But there was no attempt at censorship. I am now putting together in my mind the next book of a Northwest revolutionary trilogy which will be even more politically daring, since it will deal with the nuts and bolts of the actual Northwest revolution. *[A Distant Thunder.]* Be interesting to see whether that one finally sends up any red flags.

I might also point out that no less a personage than Antiwar.com's Justin Raimondo has been compelled to take his own book on the events of 9/11, which names Israel as a co-conspirator, to iUniverse for publication after having been rejected even by "fringe" Establishment publishers on the left and right, because of the explosive and dangerous content of the book. Apparently iUniverse isn't afraid to take on even Izra-hell, which is something we need to take note of.

My First Half Century

I honestly never thought I'd make it this far. On Sunday, September 14th, rather to my surprise, I turned fifty years of age. I am now officially a codger. If I should make it to age sixty I'll be promoted to curmudgeon, and at seventy I will attain the ultimate right wing accolade of coot. Crazy old coot, if I'm especially good at it.

Jesus! A whole half century since I appeared on this earth! Some days I feel like I'm a hundred, and some days it seems like the twinkling of an eye. But that's probably just senility setting in.

Any man who reaches my age and tells the world, "If I had it all to do over again, I wouldn't change a thing" is either a damned fool or a damned liar. Off the top of my head, I can think of a dozen things I would have done differently. But I didn't. There is no such thing as a time machine, and I have learned the hard way, through trying it a couple of times, that you can never go back. That having been said, the fact remains that I chose this life of racial service and I have no right to complain. There were a number of points along the line where I could have opted out. I sometimes tell people I never had the opportunity to go to college, but that's not true. I should more accurately say that I never had any bona fide opportunity to go to college that did not involve stipulations that were utterly incompatible with any integrity and self-respect on my part. I could have gone to West Point; I was offered an appointment from the ranks, but even then I understood that I could never serve the régime and the society responsible for creating the negroid hell I went through in high school. Back in the Seventies and Eighties there were several attempts to buy me off, by my family and others, and as recently as 1991 an agent of Benny Klassen offered me a lump sum to shut up about his Beatific Buggeries, a sum sufficiently large so that I could have used it as a grubstake to flee into the night as so many Fearless Leaders from Bill

187

Wilkinson to Rick McCarty have done.

There were as well several low ebbs in the past thirty-three years, when I could have slid off the stage into obscurity and into some shit job, and the world would have forgotten about me. By choice, I never availed myself of these chances to get out of the life, and I have no reason to wail that I never got a break. I declined to take the breaks offered because to do so entailed making my peace with a world that is putrid, poisonous, and evil to its very wellsprings. One does not make peace with a loathsome disease. One does not come to accept evil as just one of those things. One does not agree to the extinction of all that has made the world beautiful and good because it's too inconvenient to do something about it.

I will spare you a long and meandering autobiography complete with timeline. One of the mental deficiencies that appear in old age is a conceited delusion that everyone on earth is waiting with bated breath to hear "how it really was," when in fact no one gives a tinker's damn how it really was. That's one of our many problems: so few of us have any real idea what and where we came from.

Leaving aside the Northwest Migration concept and my writing, upon which the jury will be out for some time, I'm the first to admit that my life has by no means been a success, as your average Joe Twelve-Pack measures success. First and foremost, I have not made oodles and oodles of money. Thank heaven that I am genuinely non-materialistic and money has never meant that much to me, beyond what I need to survive. If I had not been able to resign for good and all any aspiration for the middle-class lifestyle, God knows how things would have gone with me. Money is a tool, a means to an end and nothing more. If someone were to ask me what my greatest strength is, I would probably answer that it is my genuine disdain for material things, a character trait now virtually unknown throughout the Western world and which gives me a tremendous advantage over those materialists with mysterious funding enabling them to hire $200 per hour attorneys.

Beyond that, my life has been a string of broken marriages, false starts, dead ends—in short, the kind of life which is all too common for White males born during the Baby Boom. My involvement with the Movement didn't help, to be sure, but this is actually a typical history for people of my race and gender in the twentieth century. Most White males of my generation would actually be considered failures by the standards of our fathers or grandfathers, who by and large valued principles and family and integrity more than wealth. If I had chosen conformity, given the general breakdown of society in the past fifty years, there is no guarantee that my life would have been any better. In fact, probably not. I might be in more or less the same boat I am now, except I'd be stuck with a humongous mortgage and with child support payments so my ex-wife and her trashy toy boy could buy drugs. I and anyone who follows in my path must beware of a tendency to blame our racial involvement for negative events and objective conditions that are in fact endemic to the entire nature of the degenerate, Politically Correct society in which we live.

Diary of a Madman?

Down through the years I have sometimes been asked why I don't write my memoirs. On several occasions, rumors to the effect that I was doing so circulated in the Bowel Movement and were greeted with a frenzy of Goat Dancing; apparently the GUBU crew finds the prospect downright terrifying. I'm flattered. But there are a number of reasons why I don't do this, revolving around specific things in my past which I have no intention of ever discussing in public. There's my childhood, for example. I've spent the past thirty-three years trying to forget most of it, and I have no intention of going back there and wallowing in old mud for the titillation of Morris Dees, armchair Jewish psychologists, and other such slimy voyeurs. There is one period of my early life which, although in no way shameful or negative, carries with it a built-in controversy which would completely overwhelm and overshadow the rest of any such volume of my reminiscences. There is the occult and mystical side of my past, which again is not something that I am in any way ashamed of, but which would be very hard to mesh with the rest of the story and which would simply distract readers from the points I would want to make. Finally, there are a few incidents in my career which even today might have negative legal repercussions for myself and others. No life history written by me could ever be complete, and if an autobiography can't be complete and honest, it should not be written. So there will be no *My Life In A Looney Bin* by Harold A. Covington.

But what I can do is take this time, with the sun rising on a cool and misty Homeland morning, to share with you a few gems of wisdom I have garnered from my three decades plus in our tragic and terrible way of life.

High Points

My life has not been without its accomplishments, not least the negative but poignant accomplishments of being able to say goodbye to much of what was good and noble about our people's past. I grew up in the much-maligned Old South, in a family sufficiently well off so that I avoided the South's traditional curse of hardscrabble poverty, and I'm even old enough to remember a few White and Colored signs on the rest rooms and water fountains. I will always be thankful that I retain some fleeting childhood memories of a better way of life. I can remember the Civil War Centennial in the 1960s and being allowed to bring Confederate flags and toys and costumery to school for show and tell; today any young White boy who attempted such a thing would be expelled and find himself marked for life by ZOG at age eight, and his parents would be in trouble as well.

I saw the lands of hope and glory that were Rhodesia and South Africa, and I can say that I know, somewhat, what life must have been like under the old colonial raj of Victorian England, since our way of doing things back in Bulawayo still came from that era. In a sense I can also claim that I am a British veteran of World War Two, since all our Rhodesian Army military manuals and procedures and even training films came from that era. Not to mention those old DC-3 s in which we flew supplies to Angola in January of 1976. Finally, I have seen the old Ireland of song and story before Ireland became a colony of Nigeria. I have seen what the old Moore Street market was like before all the White faces became black. I have seen the bullet and shell-pocked frontages of Boland's Bakery and the Four Courts and the General Post Office, and smelled the coal smoke of Dublin when it was a White city and I could walk anywhere I wanted to with no fear of being attacked because of the color of my skin, because there were no bad areas in those days. I have stood in Mitre Square in London and seen it as Jack the Ripper saw it, and supped a pint in the Ten Bells.

I have been privileged to speak at length, and on more than one occasion, with men who served National Socialism and fought for the Third Reich during the holocaust of Western civilization that was World War Two. There was Johann the Fallschirmjäger from my childhood in Burlington and Greensboro. There was the old U -boat commander Captain Fenstermacher who served in both wars, my first publisher George Dietz, and the old Lithuanian that Ray Zidarich introduced me to in the bar in Marquette Park, who pulled up his shirt and showed me his SS tattoo and blood type. There was another old man in a pub in Dublin who spent the whole night knocking back pints of Guinness and telling me of his youth with the Blue Division under General O'Duffy in Spain, as well as a dozen others. I have heard for myself *wie es wirklich war,* how it really was, from the men who were there. I would trade those meetings, conversations, and friendships for nothing on earth. When it seems to you that I rant and rave to excess about the many and undeniable weaknesses of our present day "Movement," bear in mind the reason why: I have seen the real thing, talked to the real men who did the real deed…and we ain't the real thing, not by a long shot.

Don't get me wrong. There are some good memories from Our Thing as well. Foremost among them Daley Plaza, June 25th, 1978. Let me assure you, guys, you haven't lived until you have stepped out onto a baking hot square and heard the roar of 50,000 human beings who want to tear you limb from limb.

And there were some good comrades all along the way. That's one thing I do remember: in the old NSWPP, the NSPA, the CNC and CKA, we laughed a lot. Even when me and the Chicago boys were down in the basement of Rockwell Hall poking into the earth floor to see whether or not Frank Collin had any dead little boys buried down there, I remember we laughed and sang *Bobby Brown.* There were times like that, times when you had to laugh or else you'd weep. Many, many times like that. Yet despite bad patches back then, I notice that things in our community didn't get so bitter, angry, hateful and vicious until the arrival of the internet. When White people actually get together in person, physically

191

present, we can at least somewhat interact and form friendships and develop character. We can laugh when we're actually together. But these computers seem to steal our souls and leave behind nothing but the madness and hatefulness...ah, well, you can tell I am definitely heading for codgerdom, going off on rambling tangents.

All these times, places, and people are now gone, and I am very fortunate to have been among the last to glimpse them as the shadows faded into darkness, and the world of the 19th and early 20th centuries vanished.

Faults, Bad Calls, and Just Plain Bad Luck

I have no intention of mentioning, much less addressing, the many bird-brained accusations that have been leveled at me down through the years by Movement morons. But the fact is that I have indeed made my share of bad calls and I do have my faults, and I have always been surprised that none of the Goat Dancing crew ever tried using my bona fide character flaws and weaknesses against me.

One of the things my multitudinous enemies have accused me of is "always jumping around from group to group." Okay, there is a certain element of truth in this, although not as much as some other RCC personalities. Let's take a look. I was NSWPP Franklin Road from 1972 to 1976 (four years); NSPA in its various permutations from 1976 to 1981 (six years); unaffiliated from 1981 to 1988 while I was on the run in Europe from the Greensboro grand jury (seven years); Confederate National Congress 1988 to 1990 (two years); there was a very brief period with the Klan in 1990, about six months; unaffiliated from 1990 to 1994 while I put out the original *Resistance* newsletter (four years.) I never minded George Burdi and later Pierce stealing the *Resistance* title from me. Plagiarism is the sincerest form of flattery. Then I was Fearless Leader of NSWPP Mark Two 1994 to 1999 (about five and a half years.) I suppose you can also count the virtually non-existent "National Front" in 2000, the last time I listened to the "if you build it, they will come" drivel. (Wrong. If you build it, you'd better build a circus with a freak show, a roulette wheel, and a cage full of baboons, or they won't come.)

So that's what? Six political affiliations in thirty-three years, two of which were of short duration and mostly on paper? Mmmm, okay, granted, not as stable or consistent a track record as I would have liked, but to be honest, it's about average for a Movement career the length of mine. Some of the older flacks like Cliff Herrington, Art Jones and James Warner used to go through a new letterhead front every three months. William Pierce's mere two orgs in a lifetime are extremely unusual. I once ran a comparison between my career and one who is almost my exact contemporary: the Golden Child himself, Dorian Gray. I won't repeat it here, but Double Diamond came up with exactly the same number of orgs as myself, six. Plus whatever he starts up when he gets out of the hoosegow, which will make seven. Is Duke ever reproached for inconsistency or "jumping around?" Don't be silly. David Duke is teflon. Harold Covington is velcro.

The Quest for Response

But why all the jumping around on my part? Is it because I change ideologies or allegiances? Not at all. My allegiance has always been to my race and to my civilization through the National Socialism of Adolf Hitler and George Lincoln Rockwell, and my central ideology in life has always been expressed by the Fourteen Words of David Lane, even before Lane uttered them in his final speech to the jury. **"We must secure the existence of our people and a future for White children."**

I have always sought the same thing: response. There has always been one common thread running through everything that I have done. All my life, I have been desperately searching for some way to make you people out there respond to the crisis which is overwhelming our race and our civilization. During all that jumping around, I have sent out hundreds of thousands of newsletters, leaflets, and periodicals in the mail. I have hand distributed at least a hundred thousand leaflets, papers and stickers, I have contributed to several dozen websites, and since 1996 I have sent out millions of individual e-mails to every variation on a racial or NS address I could find. The overwhelming majority of this racial material simply disappeared off the face of the earth. It dropped into a void. I have no doubt that somewhere, in dusty drawers and damp basements, in cobwebbed attics and dark rear closets, there are files and boxes and stacks of old *White Carolinas* and *Excaliburs* and *NS Bulletins* and copies of *Invictus*. Someday they may fetch huge prices from collectors or feature in museums. I'm just vain enough to believe my stuff may be valuable to collectors one day, which is why I pass out signed copies of my books. Well, at least maybe they'll do someone some good.

Getting back to the subject, here are some other bad calls I've made:

*I should have broken decisively with Koehl in Rhodesia. Without exhuming 30 year-old bones, there is a possibility that Koehl, acting through a flunky, may have been at least partially responsible for the destruction of the Rhodesia White People's Party and my deportation.

*In 1980 I trusted Gerhard Lauck. Baaaaad move! Five years of work went down the drain in a matter of weeks.

*In 1981, I refused to crack down and discipline Frank and Patsy Braswell because I *liked* them. I knew they were nuts, but they had charm and they seemed to have the devil's own luck avoiding scrapes, and it never occurred to me that one day their luck would run out. It did, and they took four innocent men to prison with them as well as repaying my years of friendship by attempting to sell my skin to ZOG to save their own.

*I created the Movement Frankenstein monster of Glenn Miller;

*I threw a lot of my own good money after bad trying to salvage the NSPA long after it became clear that it was beyond salvage. I should have just cut Collin and the whole Chicago crew loose the minute the business with the little boys came out, and saved my inheritance. But you know dumb old Harold, got to try and do the right thing if it kills him, and it damned near has a couple of times.

*I left Seattle in 1995, in order to return home to North Carolina and challenge a contemptible, woman-beating coward who had been telling lies about me. This wretch subsequently ran and hid behind an attorney's briefcase after leaving his excrement on my doorstep, and he has since gone out of his way to avoid any kind of personal settling of our differences, no matter how often I have offered him such a resolution. This was one of the very few times when I lost my cool and allowed my personal feelings to affect my political judgment, and it resulted in years of lost time. I should have ignored the asshole's bobance and boasting

194

and stayed in Seattle, and converted the NSWPP Mark Two to Northwest Migration in 1995, since even then I understood that any chance of an all-America racial recovery was gone. I allowed my gut instincts to be overruled by superficial and petty personal considerations, and that's inexcusable. I was in my early forties and I damned well should have known better. Those lost years may prove irrecoverable. Where might the Northwest be now if I had started in 1995?

The point of all this is that I am not perfect, make no claim to Man of Destiny status, and finally at age 50 I have become mature enough to where I not only do not seek it, but will not accept it if offered. My youthful ambitions to see the long brown columns goose-stepping down the streets of my home town shouting "Heil Harold" are long gone. Those in this community who can make that claim are few and far between. I may be a slow learner, but there are those among us who never learn.

A Codger's Advice To The Young

Having reached codgerdom, it is now my right to offer advice to the young, and to my amazement and gratification, we do in fact have some young still with us for me to offer advice to. The first thing I want to tell you teen and twentysomething guys and gals out there is: **stay in school** and get as much education and training as you possibly can. Do not drop out no matter how wretched it is until you get that piece of paper.

Do not deface your bodies with tattoos. Do not spend your twenties and thirties swilling beer and screaming "White Power!" while working at odd jobs or sponging off the system or other people in some way. Bulletproof yourself financially. Get a trade or a marketable skill! In God's name, don't let yourself get into the situation I am in, and find yourself turning fifty years old, living in a cardboard box, and not knowing whether or not you are going to make next month's rent! Yeah, yeah, I know, all young people think they're goddamned immortal and invincible. When you're in your twenties, the looming homeless shelter may not seem like much of a threat. You figure you can always recover, always start over. Okay, that used to be true. I heard somewhere that the greatest promise of America was that of endless fresh starts. Well, let me tell you, lads and lassies, if you're White, especially White and male, you will find that your supply of fresh starts gets less and less as the years roll along and society becomes more and more "diverse" and Whites are more and more marginalized.

For Christ's sake, listen to me! Stay in school if you're there, get into school if you're not, swallow every piece of politically correct horse shit they spoon down your throat and smile while they do it, get that piece of paper, get that marketable skill, and get yourself financially bulletproofed! If you can do something skilled or technical that needs to be done, do it well, and you're willing to do it a few bucks cheaper than the next guy, then you will have a kind of freedom most of us never know, that I never knew, because no matter how you are harassed and persecuted by the Jews, eventually you will find someone willing to pay you to do it who won't give a damn what your political and racial views are, so long as you'll work cheap.

Harold's Three Major Freak-Outs

In the past thirty-three years I have lived the life, I have on numerous occasions been totally, completely, and utterly freaked out by the behavior of people who claim to be on my side and who claim to want the same things that I want. For me to list these freak-outs would run this piece to novel length. After some consideration, here are my top three mind-bogglers:

Freakout #1: You're a Mug, Harold!

The following is an excerpt from an article I wrote in 1999, when I was on the bones of my ass in Texarkana:

"….I have been asked several times over the past two months, sometimes in almost these words, 'Harold, why the hell didn't you put some of those donations away for a rainy day, so you wouldn't be in this fix now?' Well, the reason I did not do so is quite simple. Those donations were not given to me for that purpose, and for me to have done anything of the kind would have been stealing. I have made this response on several occasions and been treated to bemused wonder in return. One guy quite seriously responded, 'Okay, what's your point?'

"You see, so utterly corrupt and debased have White Americans become, even those who are racially aware, that we assume everyone else to be just as corrupt and are often genuinely surprised on the rare occasions when we run across someone who is not. Some of you people, apparently, have been giving me your deeply-appreciated financial support over the past five years fully in the expectation that I would steal part of it, and when you found out that I did not, the reaction was almost dubious and disappointed. Some of you evidently feel that you have been backing a mug, a guy who is too dumb to stick his hand into the till when he had a chance. One man told me, in so many words, 'Jesus, Harold, you're getting on into middle age and you need to take it where you find it. You should have socked some of those donations away in a little savings account somewhere. Nobody would have known, or cared.'

"Wrong. *I would have known,* and I would have cared. And the lady from South Carolina is perfectly correct in stating that I am a failure in that sense; I am too dumb to be dishonest in the Age of Clinton, when all is permitted and accepted with apathy by the yawning White blob."

That actually happened, you know. A man who was a friend of twenty years, a man who had seriously assisted both me and the racial cause on more than one occasion, a man of intelligence and character and a true comrade, revealed to me that during all the time we had known one another, he simply assumed automatically that I was stealing. Because that's just The Movement, right? And we all know there are no true White leaders, that they're all basically con men who are in it for the bucks, right? It's just a matter of finding one whose style you like and then backing him in the full knowledge that he's dishonest, and politely looking the other way and pretending you don't see his fingers in the till, *capiche?* To this day, I don't think he understands how his automatic assumption that I am a thief shattered and upset me. I didn't bother to talk to him about it. His mind was made up, and in light of the endless string of examples proving he was right about us all, why bother to confuse him with facts?

Freakout #2: The Double Diamond Phenomenon

I now quote from last December's *Don't Cry for Me, Louisiana.* My comments here apply with vigor to Duke, but with equal force to the entire phenomenon of the corrupt White Fearless Leader. "...I have spent almost all my life trying to force us all to confront uncomfortable and unpalatable truths, so I suppose it's only fair that I should be forced to confront some myself. Along with the resurrection of Glenn Miller, the employment of feminists and miscegenators by the NA, and the rampant cult of Old Benny Buttfuck, the David Duke episode is simply one more example of the reality (to me very uncomfortable and unpalatable) that our community totally lacks any ethical principles whatever, and that we are devoid of any moral basis of any kind for what we do. There are no red lines. Nothing is forbidden and all is permitted. I have come to understand and accept the fact that we as a community are completely devoid of any kind of moral or ethical compass. It doesn't surprise me or even bother me any more. This Duke thing has left me cold. Like everyone else, I simply shrug it off in my own mind. "Nyeh, that's David. We all know David." I've kind of gone numb, I guess.

"It is a fact of life that once one achieves recognized leader status in the RCC, one can literally do no wrong. One can drug young men and sodomize them on the rec room rug. One can allow one's group to be used as a listening post and provide logistics to the government for mass murder. One can testify in court at a trumped-up sedition trial. One can file baseless and malicious lawsuits. One can leave one's feces on the doorstep of critics. One can commit vandalism and petty criminality.

"One can hand over the mailing list to the FBI on demand without so much as a whisper of protest. One can promote Satanism in order to sell CDs and make money. One can shack up in a Nazi headquarters with a coffee-colored Third World mistress. One can use Party funds to pay for one's girlfriend's abortion. One can dance around bonfires with goats and naked youths. One can house and pay a generous salary to a government witness during the year while he waits to swear away the life of another White man in a ZOG courtroom. One can put up homosexual porn websites. One can be Jewish. One can be arrested in possession of an entire barn full of kiddie porn videos and magazines. One can murder a guest in one's home and disguise it as a suicide. One can have conferences where a spy for Morris Dees records the whole affair and then pretend it never happened. One can stalk women until they flee to the courts for restraining orders. One can beat one's wives bloody and force them into anal intercourse with dildoes. One's business manager can be found shot execution-style and stuffed in the trunk of a car, and no one bats an eyelash. One can appear drunk in public twenty-four hours a day. One can post soft-porn pictures of oneself in one's underwear on the internet. One can appeal for funds to pay for medical expenses for the family and then gamble it away on riverboats and trips to the Bahamas. Basically, if you're a racist 'leader' you can pretty much do whatever the hell you want to do, and none of it matters. If one is a 'leader' one is teflon. None of it sticks. It is not that our self-proclaimed Men of Destiny make some Nietzschean claim to be Ubermenschen and above the rules. There are no rules. We have pretty much made that clear."

Every single one of the things that I referred to above has been done by men who claim to be in a leadership position in the White Aryan resistance movement. In only one single case that I am aware of in the past fifty years has even one of these men been called to account by their own membership, and that was in 1981 when I and others forcibly removed Frank Collin from the NSPA and had him sent to prison for seven years. Our more usual reaction to the cesspool in the penthouse is solipsism: if we pretend that a problem doesn't exist, then it doesn't. The 2000-pound elephant of corrupt and incompetent racial leadership sits and shits in our parlor among the tea service and the doilies, but no one except me is so impolite as to refer to him. When I attempt to discuss these things with others I am told that I am "obsessed," that I am "spreading disunity," and that this kind of egregious and appalling misbehavior on the part of the men who claim to lead us in some strange way does not matter.

How can it not matter?

I'm sorry, I don't understand. Maybe it's a linguistic problem. I simply do not speak the language of total amorality. How can such things not matter? Please, someone, explain this to me. After thirty-three years I still honest to God don't understand how betrayal and cynical abuse of our movement from the top is not important. Can anyone shed any light on this for me at all?

Freakout #3: Risk-Free Revolution

There are people reading these lines right now who believe, apparently with self-induced entire sincerity, that somehow we are going to solve this tremendous crisis of civilization and remove the threat to our racial existence without spilling a single drop of our enemies' blood. Or more to the point, without sacrificing a single drop of our own.

How? How can anyone think such a thing? How can we, the most intelligent and historically knowledgeable people on earth, the people who have made most of this planet's history, not understand something that any group of South American students plotting in a café understands quite clearly? Something that Colonel Bangalla of Bungi-Bungi grasps without hesitation as he considers his coup against General Muntu? Something that every revolutionary theorist from Lenin to Hitler to Arafat simply took as a given? The Führer organized his Stormtroops before he organized the NSDAP itself. How can anyone possibly believe that somehow or other, the greatest tyranny the world has ever known will voluntarily hand state power back to the people who originally created America and humbly depart the world stage, submitting to their just punishment for the unspeakable crimes they have committed against humanity?

[Sigh...] Well, I will tell you how. It's the "C" word, the one even I am inclined to use sparingly, because even I can understand it's not helpful. Cowardice. The spirit-breaking cry of Winston Smith for the torturer of Room 101 to hurt his beloved Julia, not him, that reduced him to a fawning human wreck who licked Big Brother's feet, as do we. Our own unspoken but well understood cry to ZOG: "Take them! Take my friends, take my wife and children, take anyone but me! My house, my car, my soft cushioned sofa, my air conditioner, my cold beer and tasty salty nachos, I cannot lose them! Take him, take her, take my neighbor, O Beast! I crawl before thee, I thump my tail between my legs and piss on the floor like the whipped dog I am, take anyone but me!" That almost never spoken C word. C as in contemptible.

We are weak, timid, deathly afraid, and yet we cannot bring ourselves to confront even in our own minds the depth of our degradation. We refuse to admit to ourselves that we are cowards who scream in fear to The Beast when it comes, begging it to take anyone else but ourselves. So we develop a dozen complex, tortuous rationalizations to relieve ourselves of the moral demand that we act, while still salving our consciences and convincing ourselves with soothing psychobabble that we really are true blue and we really are part of a great struggle which for the time being must of course always be conducted with nice, safe words, never ever with deeds that might anger The Beast and make it hurt us. This is why we so fear Northwest Migration, because it offers a safe, legal way to do rather than to say, one which is even in our own personal self interest in the long run. But once that red line of action is crossed, even if it is safe and legal action, a boundary has been breached and a precedent has been set. And that terrifies us. Harold Covington has called our bluff…and he has found that it really is nothing but a bluff, and that humiliates us. And so many of you shall turn on me, because I hold up a mirror and you do not like what you see. And for some reason, even after thirty-three years, that still freaks me out. Maybe I haven't learned much after all.

The Revolutionary Tripod

There are known rules and conditions for the success of revolution, as we have learned from our entire experience of the twentieth century. I have refined these rules into something called the Revolutionary Tripod, although they are not in themselves original with me. It is absolutely vital for all of us to internalize these rules, the three objective situations without which actual governmental and societal change on the ground cannot take place. I feel so strongly about this that I am repeating them here.

1. The Party. There must be a bona fide revolutionary movement in the form of a unified fighting revolutionary Party. This movement must be devoted not towards reforming the existing system, but to seizing the state directly from the hands of the power structure and the subsequent destruction of the old order.

2. The withdrawal of the consent of the governed. Mao said that the people are the sea in which the guerilla swims like a fish. This is why we can never abandon mass propaganda and education and political work. When we finally make our move, at least a silent majority of the White population *must* support us and be willing to help us if only in the negative sense by standing aside and not helping ZOG. The population must understand who we are and why we are fighting, and that we are fighting for *them.* Any movement that attempts to fight without such support are bandits at best, and bandits are eventually run to earth.

3. Loss of the Monopoly of Armed Force. There must be the loss of the credible monopoly of armed force by the state. It must become possible to defy the oppressors' laws with impunity. Acts of insurrection and guerrilla warfare must take place, actual and serious physical damage must be inflicted on the enemy, and no one must be caught or punished for these acts. This forces the power structure into acts of atrocity and retaliation against the general population in their frustration at being unable to locate and apprehend the real guerrillas. Textbook example: today's Iraq and Palestine.

I have an advantage over the rest of you in that I have lived in countries where revolution has taken place within living memory. I know it can be done. Remember, I have seen it and lived it in Ireland and Rhodesia. If I have one single message for all of you, it is this: *it can be done.* Not easily. Not painlessly. But *it can be done.*

An Organism, Not an Organization

For the foreseeable future, the time of the formal organization is over. The Movement must be an organism, not an organization. I am not a Fearless Leader and do not pretend to be.

Will I ever be a Fearless Leader again? Well, one thing I have learned in the past thirty-three years is never say never. But if it ever happens, then it will be not through self-appointment, but because I am offered the job by some real-world group of real, live people who assemble physically in one place as opposed to cyber-space, under conditions where form follows function. The fighting revolutionary Party of Northwest independence, when it comes into being, must be formed from the bottom up, by real live human bodies living in the Northwest Homeland, not created as a top-down letterhead organization in the false hope that "if you build it, they will come." I have built it before, and you didn't come.

The Coming of Stasis

Now that *The Hill of the Ravens* is in print, there are a few more things I need to take care of over the next couple of months, and then for all practical intents and purposes, I'm done.

By that I mean I will have reached a kind of stasis, the point where one man, all alone, without help and without resources, can do no more and should not be asked to do so. People, this Northwest Migration thing is *it*. I have neither the inclination nor the energy to dabble with it for a while and then wander off again looking for something new to which you will respond. I'm too old now. For me, for the Movement, for the White race in North America, Northwest Migration is *it*. The concept has to move forward, and it can no longer move forward as a one-man band. I've pulled my rabbit out of the hat now. I'm not "retiring" in any way...you don't retire from this madness, the Jews won't let you. Ask Ernst Zündel. But all alone, with no money, no equipment, no working space, very limited computer skills, the smallest mailing list in the RCC, and beset by all the usual problems of Movement GUBU, there simply isn't much more I can do. Except sit here for the next fifty years in a kind of twilight zone, churning out newsletters and e-mails and waiting for people who most likely will Never come. *The Hill of the Ravens* is a fantasy. I understand and accept that in the real world, there is every possibility that The Boys Of The Old Brigade will be a no-show. And that's a pity. Because we really could, you know. We Aryans can do anything we want to do, when we care enough. For fifty years, we haven't cared enough, despite everything I could do or say.

Well, who knows? Maybe another fifty will turn the trick. - HAC

www.ingramcontent.com/pod-product-compliance
Lightning Source LLC
Chambersburg PA
CBHW031509270326
41930CB00006B/328